SIEGFRIED HERFORD

Siegfried Herford on Castle Naze

SIEGFRIED HERFORD
An Edwardian Rock-climber

Keith Treacher

 THE ERNEST PRESS

Published by The Ernest Press 2000
© Keith Treacher 2000

A CIP catalogue record for this book is available
from the British Library

ISBN 0 948153 52 0

This book is dedicated to the memory of
Paul Francis Adams, who was in at the start,
but was not allowed the time to fulfil his part of it.

The photograph on the front cover shows Siegfried Herford astride the
Great Flake in July 1913

Type-set from the author's disk by Stanningley Serif
Produced by Colorcraft

CONTENTS

ACKNOWLEDGEMENTS

I owe a debt to the Fell & Rock Climbing Club for permission to quote from their Journals and in particular to George Watkins for his scholarly help; the Ladies Scottish Climbing Club (Christina Macnair); the Climbers' Club (John Neill); the Alpine Club (Margaret Ecclestone, Librarian); the Rucksack Club (John Llewellyn); the Royal Regiment of Fusiliers (J. P. Kellcher, Chief Clerk and Archivist); the School of Engineering, University of Manchester (Professor J. D. Jackson); the Hermann Lietz-Schule (Herr Ulrich Kindscher); the Cycle Touring Club, Godalming.

Vin T. Dillon responded eloquently to my request for an account of the first ascent of Extinguisher Chimney. Mrs Dorothy Joyson, sister to the late A. W. (Alf) Bridge, has entrusted her brother's unpublished poem, *Commando,* to the Rucksack Club archives and I am grateful for being able to use it.

W. G. (Bill) Bardsley took up-to-date photographs of Herford's High Peak routes; Richard Jewell drew a sketch of Central Buttress; Mrs Gwyneth Lipstein assisted through the late Paul Adams; Richard Renold went to great trouble to supply me with a genealogy explaining the connection between the Herfords and the Renolds; Walter Riley used his encyclopaedic knowledge of Manchester to help me with historical background and took me on a guided tour of Didsbury; Ian Roper supplied me with details of Herford's grave; Henry Ruff translated from the German; Christopher Sansom granted permission for use of his father's photographs; Austin Whittaker enthralled me with stories of his early days with Herford; and Eric Wild educated me on the finer points of Unitarianism.

The following gave valuable help; Shirley Angell. Tom Anderson, Peter Benson, Vin Birtles, Margaret Chapman, Trevor Collins, Rob Fergusson, Jeremy Goring, Ian Grant, Alan Hankinson, and Peter Sansom.

I record my thanks to Michael Taylor and my brother Graham Treacher who, along with my nephew Dominic Treacher, read and improved an early version of the manuscript. Peter Hodgkiss of The Ernest Press has 'fathered' the book into life. Linda Jewell not only did her valiant best to drag me into the computer age, but generously went to enormous trouble to transfer my old-fashioned typescript onto disk.

AUTHOR'S NOTE

This book owes an enormous debt to the generosity of Ralph, Theodore (Ted), and Kit Braunholtz, whose mother, the late May Braunholtz, was Siegfried Herford's sister. They have been staunch in support from the start, filling me in on various aspects of family background, correcting, adding their own perceptive comments, and putting up with my innumerable delays with stoic patience. They entrusted to my care an invaluable collection of family letters, notebooks, and other memorabilia, then extended *carte blanche* so that I could deploy sources according to my judgment. While this has meant that I have been able to include a considerable amount of hitherto unpublished material, I wish to stress that this ought not to be construed to mean that they, or any other member of the family, concur with my interpretation of events; interpretations or mistakes are my sole responsibility. What their generosity has done, however, is to shed fresh light on their remarkable uncle.

8

LIST OF ILLUSTRATIONS

L to R: Sansom,Gibson & Herford on the Girdle Traverse

INTRODUCTION

Siegfried Herford was undoubtedly the finest British rock-climber operating immediately prior to the First World War. He ranks as one of the greatest rock-climbers Britain has ever seen. Walt Unsworth, a sound judge on such matters, went so far as to describe him as 'the incomparable'.[1]

It is fair to say that Siegfried Herford has not received the attention his achievement or reputation deserves. Very little has been written about him. His name can be found in rock-climbing guides, especially the first ascent list of the Scafell guide, but we are not told anything about him. There are a few articles devoted to him, and he gets a mention in various histories of rock-climbing, but the information about him is sparse and repetitive. There has been no previous biography devoted to him.

I freely admit that until I started the research for this book, I was in the same boat as everybody else, able to quote one or two climbs he did, but knowing nothing about the man himself. It has taken me three years before I have felt confident enough to say I know a little more about him. Even now some of the true Siegfried remains shrouded in the deepest obscurity. When I reflect on it, this is hardly surprising, for during his own lifetime he was far from easy to get to know, with a distance of demeanour, content to hide himself behind a veil of self-imposed silence. I feel bound to confess that the Siegfried I have lived with for three years has emerged as infinitely complex, a strikingly powerful figure, with the laid-back arrogance of a young man aware of his own authority. Yet, although selective about the company he kept, and even then often beyond reach, one cannot help being struck by the lasting impression he left on those who met him. People spoke about him in glowing terms. *The Manchester Guardian* called him 'a man of beautiful character and great gifts'. Words like honour, courage, gentleness, and modesty, have all been used about him. He was a serious minded young man, possessed of a sharp, and well informed analytical mind, and many who looked ahead with discernment singled him out for future greatness. He had the charisma of the driven, fire in the belly, with all the intellectual and physical ability to match a surging energy.

Siegfried was barely twenty-four years of age when he was killed in the First World War. He was young in age and young in outlook, with a foot in two camps, the old and the new. One can view him as a worthy representative of his period, the epitome of the cultured and courteous Edwardian gentleman, an outstanding example of his able, chivalrous, but cruelly doomed generation. He performed in the mainstream, participating in society through established institutions, living out and safeguarding traditional values, yet at the same time he did so by projecting traditional values into the future. Much of what he did has a precursory element about it, touching ideas or movements novel in his day, even radical in a couple of instances, but which have since been absorbed by us in such a manner that we take them for granted. Adventure education is a good example of what I mean. He identified with modernising forces and was himself caught up in the transformation of the organisation of knowledge that went with them. Nowhere is this better illustrated than in his decision to become an engineer, and on top of that, the innovative direction of his research work. He held on to the past and reached out to the future.

Siegfried's high stature as a climber was acknowledged in his own day. 'Having known nearly all the finest climbers of the last thirty years' wrote W.P. Haskett Smith in 1916, 'I should be at a loss to name a single one who could be classed above Herford'.[2] History books have focused on Scafell, particularly the bold lead that resulted in the conquest of the Great Central Buttress, a landmark in homeland climbing. It was an inspired climb, indubitably, a masterful achievement, but perhaps his lasting importance extends beyond that. It has everything to do with attitude. He viewed climbing through the eyes of a climber today, and it was he, more than any other climber of his generation, who spearheaded British rock-climbing into the modern age. His legacy was not only to hand Central Buttress down to the future, but he also helped to create the future.

One of the most famous legends in British climbing centres on Siegfried. The story has it that on a bitterly cold January day a solitary climber in hobnailed boots worked his way down to Mickledore on the Scafell massif. Having reached the col, the lone climber sat for a while and began to eat lunch. As he did so a figure drifted towards him out of a thin mist lifting up from below. The figure was that of a young man, with a clear-cut face and deep blue eyes, whom the climber instantly recognised as Siegfried Herford. The two men sat together for a short spell, chatted and shared sandwiches, and then, having said their farewells, they moved off in their respective directions. The day on which this encounter is said to have taken place was January 28th, 1916, the very day on which Siegfried was killed by a German rifle grenade in the trenches of the First World War. It is ironic that a man as rational and scientific as Siegfried should be remembered by what is effectively a ghost story, evocative of his intimate association with Scafell, a reminder to us of how his presence still lingers on the mist-laden col of Mickledore.

A word needs to be added about the spelling of names. Spelling used in quotations is often likely to throw up problems. My decision has been to retain the original so long as the meaning is clear. The reader, therefore, will find Doe Crag in place of Dow Crag (there are those who insist it ought to be Doe, in any case); Llwydd will be found instead of Lliwedd. By retaining them I hope to capture the flavour of the original.

CHILDHOOD AND YOUTH

1891-1909

It is sometimes well not to grow up
too quickly; hard wood grows slowly,
and burns all the longer.

Christian Klucker

Adventures of an Alpine Guide.

CHAPTER ONE

PLANET MARS

Siegfried Wedgwood Herford was born on July 29th, 1891, in a tall Victorian house with all the appurtenances of the well-to-do middle class. The building stood on the bracken-strewn cliff above the promenade at Aberystwyth and in full view of Constitution Hill.

The new addition to the family found himself christened with names that reflected his parents' strong sense of family roots. The Teutonic Siegfried, so reminiscent of Wagner's *Nibelungenlied*, followed naturally from his mother's German nationality. Wedgwood, by contrast, indicated the family link with Josiah Wedgwood, the potter manufacturer and Captain of Industry. His forebears in the paternal line, strong-willed people, hardy and thrifty, with a tenacity of belief in the justice of their own cause, trace back to Devon and Somerset. The original spelling of the surname was almost certainly Hereford. [1]

Siegfried's background was of a kind to give any growing boy confidence in himself. Culture and learning were of the essence. A family tradition had it that one Nicholas Herford had assisted Wycliffe in the translation of the Vulgate into English; the story might well not be true, but it is characteristic.

Siegfried's birthplace at Aberystwyth was determined by the fact that his father held the Chair in English Language and Literature at the University College of Wales.[2] Professor Charles Harold Herford was a man of singularly charming disposition and even temper. One of his grandsons, Ted Braunholtz, used the word 'adorable' when describing him. The late Mrs Gwyneth Lipstein, of Cambridge, remembered him affectionately as 'a darling, very sweet and gentle'. He was a quaint figure, professorial in appearance, rather like the benign uncle who suddenly pulls faces and frightens the children.[3] Quaint he might have appeared, but there was nothing quaint about his high reputation as a scholar, being reckoned 'the most accomplished English scholar of his age'.[4] He was known to everybody as 'the Professor' and that is how we shall know him in this book. The Professor's home at Aberystwyth was a scholar's den, reeking of morocco-bound books, and from the moment the young Siegfried romped about the uplands outside his front door he inhaled the oxygen of culture and learning.

Behind the solid and secure lifestyle at Aberystwyth stood Siegfried's mother, a remarkable lady in her own right, and mother and son were to

Siegfried playing the violin

BOX RULES ARE ONLY TO SHOW POSITION

Siegfried's father and mother (Both drawings by Siegfried's sister)

evolve a warm and intimate relationship. Marie Catherina Herford, *née* Betge, was the daughter of the Chief Postmaster of Bremen, Germany's oldest port. It was common for somebody like herself, born and bred into the German bourgeoisie, to be given a sound grounding in music and literature. The heavy formality of her class, together with the restricted expectation which confined her, conflicted with her strong independence of mind. She was open to fresh ideas and was not beyond toying with radical notions about the nature of society or the aims of education. She was to escape from Bremen by taking up a teaching post in Manchester, which is how presumably she and the Professor first met. She was not to know it, but climbing history would have a strange irony in store for her in the shape of Colin Kirkus. Kirkus, regarded by many as Siegfried's rightful successor as a rock-climber during the 1930s, revered Siegfried as a model. While a serving Pilot Officer in the RAF, Kirkus was killed in September, 1942, when engaged on a bombing raid over Bremen, the home city of his hero's mother. But before that could happen, however, Marie Herford would have her own war and her own tragedy to come to terms with.

Siegfried had a sister two years older than himself. Strictly, her name was Mary, but for some reason or another the name never stuck, and she was addressed as May by everybody. Again, that is how we shall know her.

May was to become a lady of intelligence and sensitivity who inherited much of her father's sweetness of character and equally much of his literary and linguistic propensity. When a Classics lecturer at the University of Manchester, during the reign of the redoubtable R.S.Conway, she wrote the authoritative *Introduction to the Study of Greek Vase Painting,* published by the Manchester University Press, 1919. Gilbert Murray, in a letter to her *(July 30th, 1919)*, acclaimed it 'the most attractive of the Vase books'. A quality of constancy has been attributed to May, in the sense that she was always the first to act when a member of the family or a friend had need of support, and there is ample evidence to show how she actively backed up Siegfried behind the scene. She was a strong person, never an easy target, well capable of holding her ground in an argument. She confessed on one occasion that she shared the streak of stubbornness common to all Herfords, which was no bad thing, for it held her in good stead when she was in a campaigning mood on the behalf of some point of social justice. She was stubborn, for instance, in 1911 when she declared her support for Keir Hardie and his striking railwaymen who had barricaded Exchange Station in Manchester. She was stubbornly angry when the Government sent in the troops in an effort to smash the barricade; it only served to confirm her view that the Government had completely failed to understand what had caused the strike in the first place. Her practical care at an individual level, coupled with her strong social idealism, was enhanced by a thought-through Christian belief. Being a Herford, she was of course a cradle Unitarian, but she underwent a theological change of mind and joined the Church of England. In 1922, May married Gustav E.K.Braunholtz, Professor of Comparative Philology and a Fellow of Worcester College, Oxford. Theirs was a long and happy marriage from which there were three sons and a daughter.

Siegfried and May spent eight years of a secure and happy childhood together at Aberystwyth. The sensuous vitality of the Welsh countryside, the shivering light of hill and sea, fed their active and fertile imaginations. A mysterious landscape lay all around them, alive and permeated with the magic of childhood, the land of the *Mabinogion* populated with innumerable mythical beasts and strange creatures, from the giant Ysbadden to the uncanny Culweh. At any time on a family walk around their local hills they were liable to bump into one of these fascinating creatures. It was a consolidating atmosphere and by sharing their imaginary world together brother and sister sealed a lasting bond. May explained how it came about and how Siegfried grew to become her ideal comrade:

> It began, for me, when as children we planned, peopled and described an imaginary world. We were kings of two closely allied countries, situated on the planet Mars; we consulted together on affairs of state, we swore oaths of loyalty to one another, and the very mountains of our respective lands was honour bound not to exceed one another in height. Into this very adaptable world we imported every new experience which life brought to one or other of us; it was to Siegfried that battle stories, languages, submarines, cricket, mountain-maps owed their vivid counterparts in Mars; and in all these ventures he made me his partner from the start. [5]

This inordinately adaptable world on planet Mars was further supplemented by a love of word play. W.A. Darlington, one-time drama critic on *The Daily Telegraph*, wrote: 'They were clever children, May and Siegfried. I remember a party at their home at which each child was presented with a special set of verses composed in his or her honour by the young hosts.' [6]

They revelled in creativity of that kind. May wrote charming little stories which sometimes served as Christmas presents for Siegfried or her parents. Siegfried composed verses, often accompanied by a sketch, dubious masterpieces reminiscent of Edward Lear, and all carefully signed with his nickname, Seaweed. Even at this early stage in their lives, the children were bilingual, well capable of expressing themselves in their mother's native tongue, and several of the pieces written around that time are in German.

Aberystwyth was a time of golden days, a halcyon period of secret childhood tête-à-têtes, of messing about on the beach, or Siegfried charging 'Poop-poop' along the Prom. Planet Mars belonged to the infectious realm of the imagination and it must have seemed to both children that time had stood still and the two of them would stay kings of their closely allied countries for ever. Yet it has to be added that it was not entirely an idyll. Under the kindergarten surface there were hints, no more than that, but pointers to suggest that all might not be plain sailing once Siegfried reached his boy years. Occasionally, life on planet Mars would be interrupted by feelings of aggression or fits of anger. They were there, these signs and portents, but never strong enough to overshadow the magic. May and Siegfried were always to find that Aberystwyth drew the soul.

CHAPTER TWO

DIDSBURY AND UNITARIANISM

1901 saw the Professor appointed to the newly-created Chair in English Literature at the University of Manchester. It was a clear indication of just how far his stature as a scholar had moved forward.

The Professor was a Manchester man by birth, his father having run a successful business as a wine-merchant in the city, and obviously the new Chair demanded a return to his native roots. Siegfried would have to leave his own birthplace in Wales. Every member of the family, and particularly so the children, found putting Aberystwyth behind them an enormous wrench. We can only surmise the emotion they felt when the final moment came to bid adieu to the much loved house, the home of planet Mars.

The area of Manchester the Professor and Marie Herford selected for their new home was Didsbury. Didsbury, from the family's point of view, proved an ideal choice. It was a growing middle-class oasis in an otherwise bleak industrial landscape, with all the signs of developing into a University enclave, one of those residential areas which underlined the gap between splendour and squalor common to industrial cities based on a *laissez-faire* economy. Didsbury boasted spacious houses in marked contrast to the poky hovels with their soot-encrusted flues. The new Herford home lay outside the permanent pall of smog that hovered over the mills and dye-works and tanneries, a blessing for the Professor who suffered regular bouts of asthma. The family timed their arrival perfectly. They moved in at the time Didsbury surrendered its dependence on the horse-drawn omnibus for access to the city centre; the first electric tram departed Albert Square on June 1st, 1901. Electric trams were a measure of the changes Manchester was undergoing, yet even so, Didsbury's streets were still lit by gas lamp, errand boys whistled their favourite music-hall tunes as they delivered goods to the posh houses, beer in a pub was pegged at 2d a pint, and tobacco could be had for 3d an ounce.

The new family home at 5 Parkfield Road was a large building designed to the Professor's own specifications – as a young student he had trained to become an architect – and constructed by the local firm of Burgess and Galt. There was ample accommodation for everybody, the children, a cook, a live-in housemaid, together with sufficient guest rooms to cater for the many representatives from the academic world who came to stay. On the left of the main entrance, jutting onto a lawn, the Professor had designed a bow-shaped tower, a sort of Germanic touch, the basement of which contained his study. This was territory out of bounds to the children. Building a house in Didsbury at the turn of the century meant plenty of land for a substantial garden. The garden at Parkfield Road, a section of which is now adjacent to the Northern Tennis Club, contained a wide lawn, extensive flower beds, and a plentiful spread of fruit trees.

The garden was very much Marie Herford's domain. On those occasions when her son used it for letting off steam, however, she must have thought it a mixed blessing. Austin Whittaker, a contemporary of Siegfried's in the early Didsbury days, recalled in an interview the boyish shenanigans which took place. He remembered with an understanding twinkle how Siegfried, 'with that superb body of his, you know', could sometimes be 'a bit wild'. He recounted how Siegfried, baying grunting noises like a gorilla, clambered up an apple tree. Once safely on top he began to fling apples in all directions with total abandon. It was a typical outburst of uncontrolled energy. One whizzing missile landed with a resounding thud on his mother's face, narrowly missing a serious cut, but badly bruising her left eye. It was, added Mr Whittaker, the only time he saw the Professor lose his temper.

One distinct advantage of the move to Didsbury was that it restored the family's contact with the mainstream of the Unitarian Church. They had not been entirely cut off from Unitarianism in Aberystwyth. The Meeting House in the middle of town had not as yet been acquired, but, from 1895 onwards, a small group met for worship in the library of G.Eyre Evans. It was better than nothing, but hardly what the Herfords were looking for, the closely-knit Welshness getting in the way of their cosmopolitan outlook.

This is perhaps the best moment to draw back and take a look at the word Unitarian. The Herford family in general were active in the Unitarian cause and it was one of the key formative influences on Siegfried himself. He grew up surrounded by bearded Unitarian uncles and refined aunties, confident and self-assured, regarding the world 'steadily and whole'. Principal Raymond Holt has pointed out the way Unitarians at the time viewed themselves as 'the Vanguard of the Age'.[1] The Herfords were no exception.

Unitarians trace their church history back to the Reformation. A church dictionary defined Unitarianism as: 'A type of Christian thought and religious observance which rejects the doctrine of the Trinity and the Divinity of Christ in favour of the unipersonality of God'.[2] In a strict sense, the definition is fair, for that is how Unitarianism goes back in history. But history has also seen big changes of belief and outlook come about, particularly in the last century, so that today few Unitarians would give that dictionary definition of themselves. The dictionary stress on doctrine is now replaced by an emphasis on the spirit. This is even true of a great deal of the Unitarianism to be found in Siegfried's day. The Unitarian ethos Siegfried inherited certainly had a strong theological stress to it, but in essence it was more about an attitude of mind in religion, the central place of reason, the importance of tolerance, the freedom of each person to believe as mind, heart or conscience dictate. One of his uncles, the Revd. Doctor Brooke Herford, well illustrated the outlook of his day: 'The One, Infinite Father-life, without any confusing subtleties about inner relations of His being; the dignity of human nature, as something not hopelessly lost and ruined, but ever advancing as the ages pass'. The fervent belief in the dignity of Human Nature proved an important aspiration in terms of social action. In all the big cities of the land, Unitarians were at the helm of reforms in industry, local government, housing and public health. Education was nothing less than a passion; Manchester University, where the Professor had been appointed to a Chair, being itself a Unitarian foundation.

Didsbury allowed easy access to Fallowfield and Platt Unitarian Chapel, under the incumbency of the Revd. William Whittaker – Austin Whittaker's father – who became a close family friend. The Revd. Whittaker espoused the 'Social Gospel' in a forceful manner, a Gospel not dissimilar to the one held by the Herfords themselves.[3] What particularly attracted the Professor and Marie Herford was the German strain in the theology they found. Platt Chapel was one of the Unitarian establishments where the Tübingen School of New Testament theology, founded by Ferdinand Baur under the influence of Hegel, was granted a willing pulpit.

Both Siegfried and May became regular attenders at Platt Sunday School, in those days housed in a separate building. As she grew older, May would occasionally assist at the Sunday School, an exercise not always free of hazard as she explained in a letter to her father who was working at the time in Norway:

> At Sunday School this afternoon (it was a short service held in the Chapel) Mr Whittaker addressed an audience of 10 children and 2 teachers!! For the want of anyone else, I had to play the organ!! Mr W. came up with me and we experimented together on the stops, trying to produce a suitable tone – and after three notes, each with a different stop, there came, not a fourth note – but a great nothing. So we began over again, and having found a suitable combination

of stops, left them severely alone, and I played the hymn through in a martial fashion, and without any expression at all.

May, in later years, even after she had converted to Anglicanism, kept up her friendship with the Revd. Whittaker and continued to retain an affection for the old Chapel.

Siegfried's direct relationship with Unitarianism is not quite so clear. There is nothing to show, for instance, that he took a leaf out of his sister's book and actually took charge of a Sunday School class, although we have his own authority for saying that he did attend the occasional Sunday service at Platt Chapel during his student days at Manchester University. It is difficult to come to a fair judgment as to how far his Unitarian upbringing held firm as he grew older. It is quite certain that he did not follow the same path as his sister by turning to an orthodox theological position; if anything, the indications are that he travelled in the opposite direction. Various scraps of paper, and scribbled references here and there, suggest his mind had gravitated to a nominal ethical humanism, a strand in the liberal tradition that has placed the notion of God in the same category as gnomes and fairies, the 'God is dead' culture as old as the Golden Bough of Nemi. Having said that, it is impossible to say how far he might have sided with Protagoras when he declared 'Man is the measure of all things'. Siegfried's strong moral idealism owed a direct debt to his Unitarian roots, and as he matured, clarifying his own beliefs, he went on to give his personal interpretation of the debt he felt.

The family quickly settled down at Parkfield Road. Marie Herford possessed a marvellous gift for transforming a house into a home, generating an air of order and security, creating the right climate which enabled the Professor to study and write, and the children to grow up in their own way. With an active social life, cultural societies to attend, music and theatre, philanthropic endeavour, together with boundless visitors to the house, there was always plenty to do. The Didsbury Herfords were a family who liked to get involved. Sometimes, both parents and children thought back wistfully to Aberystwyth, and the absorbing times they had enjoyed there, but life had moved on. Parkfield Road would come to have the utmost importance for Siegfried: it was from there that he organised his climbing expeditions and it was from there that he would go to war.

*Siegfried aged nine at
Lady Barn House School*

The one-time Lady Barn House School   Photo: Walter Riley

CHAPTER THREE

QUIT YOU LIKE MEN

The tangled web of Siegfried's school days brings to the fore aspects of his character while at the same time underlining a number of cultural and social forces which combined to fashion him. There was little that was easy about his education. He did not follow the well-oiled groove from prep school to public school, but instead he was sent to a variety of institutions, each with its own distinctive view about the ultimate aim of education, each adopting its own method of teaching, a conflux of philosophies and expectations in conflict with one another. This was not a deliberate policy on the part of his parents. Almost from the time he attended his first school, the problems which had begun to surface at Aberystwyth dictated the tortuous path Siegfried would follow.

One small detail needs to be referred to. The reader will notice that the dates on which he attended his first school makes clear that he was already boarding in Manchester before the family came to make their break with Aberystwyth. This must have done a lot to cushion the settling-in process once Parkfield Road was opened. He would already have made some friends of his own age.

Siegfried's first school was Lady Barn House, located, when he joined in 1899, in a large Victorian building in the Mauldeth Road, in what is now the suburb of Withington. Today it is a successful school at Cheadle in Cheshire. The stretch of land west of the school was still open country but increasingly under the threat of encroachment from a rapidly expanding city. The village of Lady Barn itself acquired the nickname 'Soapsud Island' owing to the large number of women who took in washing. Siegfried was a boarder from 1899 to 1901, after which he became a day-boy until 1903. Lady Barn House not only reflected the Unitarian ideas which permeated Siegfried's home life, but it was in a very real sense an extension of the family, being founded in 1873 by Siegfried's great-uncle William Henry Herford.

William Henry Herford, a gifted and inventive man of phenomenal energy, served for a time as the Unitarian minister at Lancaster. It was during his ministry there that he was approached by Lady Noel Byron, widow of the poet, who asked him to act as tutor to the eldest son of her daughter, the Countess of Lovelace. The commission evolved taking the boy to a school at Hofwyl on the outskirts of Bern, run by the impressive Swiss-

German patrician Wilhelm Von Fellenberg. [1] Hofwyl was a school based on the radical theories of Friedrick Froebel and it completely changed the direction of William Henry Herford's life. He was stunned by what he saw and determined to spend the rest of his life practising and propagating Froebel's ideas. On his return to Lancaster he established Castle Howell School in 1850, along Froebelian lines, first in West Place and later in Queen Square after the school prospered. Subsequently, following the surrender of his interest in Castle Howell, he moved back south to Manchester and started up Lady Barn.

Lady Barn House typified the expectations of a group of people who thought carefully about educational matters and it attracted the sort of liberal intelligentsia to which the Herfords belonged. It represented a distinct break from the general run of preparatory schools. For such a radical school to succeed, or even survive, it depended upon active support and large pockets of like-minded people. Here the strong German community then prominent in the cultural and business life of Manchester enthusiastically came forward. W.C.R.Hicks, in his history of the school, made a special point of singling out the German factor:

> From the very beginning, parents who were either German themselves or of German extraction, sent their children to Lady Barn, and in many cases their descendants have followed their example. Of the 111 pupils who entered the school during the first ten years of its existence, no less than 42 bore German names. [2]

This accurately reflects the Herford position. They not only sent their son and daughter to the school, but they had close ties with the German community on a cultural and social level, a community established enough to support its own Lutheran Church in Wrights Street and sponsor a mainstream Anglo-German High School for Girls.

At the time William Henry Herford was busy setting up his two schools, Castle Howell and Lady Barn, the preparatory and public school sector was beginning to find the pressure of examinations, both competitive and qualifying, more unavoidable. Examinations were increasingly demanded 'at the points of entry to the money-making occupations deemed socially most eligible'. [3] William Henry Herford had not the slightest intention of having anything to do with such utilitarian notions. Education for him was about the child, the whole child, and not the demands or requirements of the professions, or trade, or industry. No one was firmer in his mind about the distinction between education and training. He had a perfectly clear idea about what he meant when he offered parents 'a sound classical education' for their offspring. It was a concept Siegfried's parents thoroughly approved of.

William Henry Herford's schools were founded on the proposition that a child's energy contains its own volition, in the sense of a spontaneous commitment to life, and a curiosity about life. *How* a child learns matters a great deal more than *what* it learns. Rather than any concentration on the extent of knowledge, there has to be a thoroughness of intellectual effort, each child's mind being enlarged by what it feeds on. Intellectual effort, on the other hand, must be offset by regular physical activity, by plenty of fresh air, supplemented by a routine of exploratory play designed to enhance a child's sense of being in the world and not outside it.

Undoubtedly, the manner in which a school governed itself was at the very heart of the institution, for this above all else determined its ethos and tone. It was crucial to establish a mechanism of genuine, if rudimentary self-government, one which assured a real reciprocity between staff and pupil. At Lady Barn this was called 'a small Commonwealth'. This, by definition, ruled out any form of imposed authority. Punishment was ruled out, and never used at the school, and even minor forms of admonition were actively discouraged. The same philosophy set out to eradicate competitiveness in all its forms, whether it be for merit-marks a child might earn in class or a prize won in a game. Lady Barn House just about allowed itself to tolerate team games, and even took part in interschool matches, but they were quite clear that prizes only served to encourage vanity. Everything at the school, whether intellectual activity, internal school government, or taking part in sport, had as its aim the enlargement of a child's potentialities for personal fulfilment and social usefulness, and nothing would be allowed to frustrate that.

How well or badly did Siegfried do at Lady Barn?

The evidence suggests that particularly during the first two years at the school, perhaps significantly when he was a boarder, he got along reasonably well and showed some encouraging progress.

He acquired a fondness for carving in wood and by the end of his second year he was proficient enough to carve Christmas presents for his parents and sister; he started a stamp collection, as boys tend to do, and he badgered his parents to send him all their foreign stamps; his violin playing shot ahead by leaps and bounds, although a sketch of him at this period showed he was having difficulty sitting correctly, not an uncommon fault among boys, and there is an urgent plea to his mother for a fresh batch of German songs; Shakespeare's plays fired his imagination and we find him writing a long letter home explaining to his father the plot of *The Merchant of Venice* (the Professor, who had edited the monumental Eversley Shakespeare, was no doubt grateful for his son's help!). On parents Open Days, Siegfried showed little inclination to act, preferring to hide behind his accustomed silence, but he could be generous about the performing efforts of his friends. During his third year we see the start of a love of bird-life, a passion he would retain throughout his climbing career. One minor disappointment came his way when he badly wanted to travel to London to see Queen Victoria's funeral and was not allowed to go.

Behind all the outward signs of progress being made, however, things were far from well. The plain truth of the matter is that Siegfried was an unhappy boy at odds with himself and just about everything around him. He was always a silent boy. A late letter from 'Aunt Gussie' to May (February 22nd, 1932) recalled his early days, how he would sit 'at table opposite to me with downcast eyes that would be suddenly lifted and that would smile at one in silent reference to some comment or other made at table'. Now, at Lady Barn House, the eyes had stopped smiling and the silence had grown disconcerting, threatening, almost a gazing dumbness. Something was very clearly wrong. On one occasion the Professor, speaking of his son's education, vaguely referred to what he called Siegfried's 'special needs', 'vaguely' because he did not go on to explain what they were. There is no cause to exaggerate the special needs, or to magnify them into some form of psychological bogey, but we have to acknowledge that behind them lay a powerful disturbance remorselessly forcing its way to the surface. The silences took on a grudging edge, indicating a very real tension, and the fact that the boy was so much at odds with himself was a problem for both his parents and the school. A firm check would need to be kept on what was happening.

The kernel of Siegfried's problem, the root cause of his special needs, lay in the sheer intensity of the life force within him, an almost terrifyingly active drive, a predisposed energy that would dominate the gamut of emotions. Nature had bestowed upon him munificent gifts in the form of two powerful tendencies, an acute intelligence coupled with a physicality that was almost rampant. On the surface he was blessed, but during those moments when each tendency failed to operate in tandem, refusing, for whatever reason, to act in harmony, he faced periods of inner clamour hard to endure.

Siegfried's mind sometimes had such an ultra-active buzz about it that he ran away with himself. A brilliant analytical facility would eventually find a natural home for itself in mathematics. In fact, mathematics came early. The Professor recalled how even as a toddler, Siegfried displayed a keen interest in numbers, so that when they wandered about the local Aberystwyth hills the allurement of distant peaks had always to be supplemented by precise statistics of their height, compared with Mount Everest or any other mountain he had heard of. If, for whatever reason, this facility was starved he became bored, withdrawing behind an unbearable silence which left him scarcely able to muster enough of himself to make contact with other human beings. In company he would lapse into silence without so much as a flicker of recognition; it was almost as if there was nobody there. In parallel with an ultra-active mind he had also to carry an ultra-active body. Austin Whittaker had described his body as 'superb'; Geoffrey Winthrop Young was to notice how 'from his knee to his shoulder there looked to be a single powerful spiral of muscle.'[4]; one of his mother's friends called him a 'Sun-God'. It was all magnificent, of course, but if ever a young boy had a problem with his body, it was Siegfried. His physical energy had the force of a cataract hurling on the flood, but when thwarted, as sometimes happened, it would burst out of control. His sister May wrote: 'His superabundance of physical energy would often express itself in outbursts of impetuous violence'.[5] These outbursts had nothing to do with violence per se; they were more akin to feelings of rage enabling him to efface a sense of powerlessness that raw energy can engender. But when the outbursts came they struck like a whirlwind taking all before it.

The Professor was badly placed to confront a growing problem. The absentee father was at the best of times a common feature of Edwardian middle-class life. The Professor was particularly prone to it, for the more his reputation as a scholar grew so the demands on his time proportionally increased. He was called upon to lecture, to attend conferences, to meet and converse with fellow scholars, whether at home or just as likely abroad, and it so often meant that when Siegfried needed him he was not there. There is a letter from Siegfried asking his father to turn up for an event at school. But there was a problem – the Professor was away at the time on a visiting lectureship in Boston USA. In reply, Siegfried got a description of a visit to the Niagara Falls:

> It was just a week ago I was there – a glorious May day. You know the great broad river comes rushing along from Lake Erie, and before it gets into the next Lake, Ontario, it has to fall downstairs whether it will or not – 160 feet – in one great plunge altogether.

It was worthy geography, perhaps, but in the following sentence he had to tell his son bluntly that the heavy demands of work would not permit him to spend time at school on his return to England. Siegfried had to come to terms with the fact that he had a gentle and brilliant scholar for a father, fully absorbed in a noble world of his own, a world of Germanic and Nordic culture, and he was going to have to fight his own battles. No fatherly neglect was intended and nor was there any irretrievable breakdown in the relationship. Mutual love, care, respect and pride textured a complex relationship, and also trust, but there was distance and sometimes tension in a filial bond that lacked the warmth of intimacy.

The Professor's precarious position in relation to Siegfried's special needs was further compounded by the inabilities of the family-packed staff at Lady Barn House. The uncomfortably prolonged silence, interspersed with fits of impetuous violence, proved beyond the comprehension or skill of staff. There was no opportunity to stand away. The school was too much of a Herford coterie; there were Herfords in charge; Herfords teaching; Herfords on the committee; Herfords forever popping in and out. In a claustrophobic and inward-looking atmosphere, in which Siegfried was designated an awkward member of the family rather than a difficult pupil, no objective assessment could be made. The upshot was that a collision between the two drew inexorably closer as term succeeded term.

The rapidly worsening situation at Lady Barn House obviously confronted Siegfried's parents with an unpalatable dilemma. They were proud of Siegfried, proud of the school, and it meant a great deal to them to have him there. They gave their backing to the school with the conviction of true believers. Both fervently espoused Froebel's aim as expounded in his 1826 masterpiece *The Education of Man* (translated into English by William Henry Herford):

> Education consists in leading Man as a thinking intelligent
> being into self-consciousness, to a pure and unsullied and free
> representation of the inner law of Divine Unity and in teaching
> him the ways and means thereto.

They held firmly to that. A belief in the inner law of Divine Unity dovetailed into their Unitarian theology. The representation of the Divine Law took on the form of a crusade, bound up with notions about the worth and dignity of each individual, the right of every child to an educated mind. In Lady Barn House they felt that they had found a school as unsullied as any was liable to be. That is why they had sent both their children there; why the Professor sat on the School Council under the Chairmanship of C.P.Scott, editor of *The Manchester Guardian*; and that is why Marie Herford drummed up financial support from the Manchester German community.

The manner in which Siegfried's parents faced up to the problem in the end says a lot about their strength of character. We have no record of their reasoning, only their decision. What they did was to opt for a traditional authoritarian school about as opposite to the libertarian mode of Lady Barn as it was possible to get. Siegfried was about to undergo a dose of muscular Christianity and cold-bath morality at its most Edwardian. It was all so thoroughly unexpected.

The drastic move took Siegfried to Boxgrove House School, a Preparatory School for Boys, in contrast to the mixed classes of Lady Barn. The school, tucked on the Surrey Downs on the outskirts of Guildford, was a place as English as the underwood of hazel and ash shading its leafy grounds. Siegfried remained there as a boarder from 1903 to 1906.

If it can be said that the ghost of Froebel hovered over Lady Barn House, then the spirit of Thomas Arnold of Rugby drifted through the gaunt corridors of Boxgrove. At the heart of the school were the hallowed cadences of the Authorised Version of the Bible and the Book of Common Prayer. All the Christian virtues were to be upheld by masters and boys alike: to be obedient and truthful and upright and industrious. The school derived its inspiration from Arnold's great sermon on *Christian Education*:

> To render the bodies of men strong and active, their minds clear, rich and versatile, and their spirits able to control both mind and body and direct their physical and mental powers to the service of God.

That was the sublime aim of education. And it pays to look carefully at Arnold's words. The key words of a sermon which denoted idealism and energy were to *control* ... to *direct* ... both *mind* and *body* ... the very thing Siegfried had found hard to do and why he had been taken away from Lady Barn. He had been unable to adjust to his natural gifts of mind and body and manoeuvre the two into a workmanlike focus. Arnold said nothing about an inner law, still less a Divine Unity. Indeed, in a very real sense, he turned Froebelism on its head, by insisting that physical and mental powers be directed outwards and not inwards, outwards to the service of an objective God, as if the secret of Man's life is to be sought in that which lies not within but without. Of course, nobody was more aware of the intractability of his task than Arnold, for the thought of human frailty was never far away, the darkness of the human soul overcoming him with mortification. He once said:

My object will be, if possible, to form Christian men, for Christian boys I can scarcely hope to make.

Nevertheless, with God on his right hand to guide him, supported by the inestimable virtue of the whipping-block wreaking expiation for the sins of youth, he had a good try.

Siegfried quickly discovered that an Arnoldian-type prep school was much given to the cult of hardness. Discipline was as strict as it was physical: the Headmaster and his staff never doubted the old adage that corporal punishment improves the moral fibre of the boy (William Henry Herford would have turned in his grave). There was a hectic daily routine with the boys kept at full stretch all the time, a sure way of avoiding 'silly thoughts', and essential so as to forestall insubordination. Siegfried himself drew a picture of what it was like in a letter he wrote home on September 27th, 1903, shortly after his arrival at the school:

> This is the history of a day. We get up at 6.45., and 3 of us go to cold baths. We then go down to the schoolroom and prepare a lesson till 7.15. Then Mr Bidden gives us a Scripture lesson till 8.00 when we have breakfast. We take 20 minutes for that, and go out into the playground, if fine, and play cricket till 9.00. Then we have les sons, mostly with Mr Bidden till 11.15, when we have a break, and then go on to 12.30. and then play cricket on the playground till 1.10. Then we have dinner, and then we read till 2.00. Then we go for a walk on the downs till 4.00., on Wednesdays till 6.00. When we come back at 4.00., we have lessons till tea time at 6.00. This lasts twenty minutes and we read till 7.00., then we have three preparations till 8.00., when we go into the dining-room, have prayers and then go to bed. We are allowed to talk till about nine; it is usually stories told by Unwick.

Mens sana in corpore sano indeed! Siegfried's somewhat breathless letter well illustrates the tightly structured life at the school. It was a very different world from Lady Barn.

Other letters in the Braunholtz collection show that Siegfried retained the Herford libertarian spark by objecting to the staff censoring his letters home (for neatness, it was said), but otherwise all the indications are that he not only settled down, but responded positively and gained a great deal from the school. Academic standards at Boxgrove House were demandingly high and he had instilled into him a habit of work he never lost. He was to do outstandingly well in mathematics and, to much rejoicing on his part, he eventually succeeded in winning the coveted Maths prize against stiff opposition. The daily walks across the Downs, with their folds and crests and the rolling Weald to the east, bred a liking for the softer undulations of the southern countryside which he would consolidate in later years. The importance of Boxgrove House School for Siegfried was not academic; he would have shone academically at whatever school he attended. The importance was an influence on him which dug a great deal deeper than scholastic achievement. It was at Boxgrove that he first encountered the notion of the elitist *noblesse oblige*, a notion so thoroughly antithetical to anything he had known at home or at Lady Barn, and, far from reacting against it, he was to imbibe it. Later, when he came under the influence of a great educationalist, he was to work on the notion and formulate his own version of it.

Boxgrove House was no exception to the run of other preparatory schools of the time, if perhaps somewhat more academic than most. The school, like the public school system in general, crystalised the British class structure as a matter of policy by calculatingly catering for a socio-élite. There was an easy assumption that the boys being educated belonged to an officer class and were the natural rulers of society as by right. The school knowingly set out to mould 'them that hereafter may be deemed worthy to be governors of the public weal'. Worthiness to exercise governorship was achieved first through submission to status and authority and then through the exercise of them. Those who ran the schools believed the system assured that the lower orders – the *peasants* Siegfried would call them – were ruled wisely and justly by leaders, the courtier, the soldier and the scholar, the type of young men Siegfried would come across again when he entered the select mountaineering circles of his day.

To acquire leadership status boys had to learn how to quit themselves like men.

There is a strong indication of Siegfried's thinking while he was at Boxgrove contained in two letters he wrote describing his reaction to a sermon preached at the school by the Headmaster, Mr Caldwell M.A. The Headmaster took as his text the ever popular *1 Samuel 4.9:* 'Be strong and quit you like Men'. Caldwell would have been well aware of the connotation attached to *Men*; in Edwardian days it was a synonym for leader. 'Be strong and quit you like Men' was tantamount to 'Be strong and quit you like a Leader'. Here is a quote from a passage of the sermon in which the Headmaster expounded on a boy's duty.

> You have a truly sacred duty to perform. It is your plain duty to prepare yourselves to fortify your bodies and your minds for the battle of life. And I often reflect upon the weakness of human – aye

boy – nature when I observe the hesitations – the shrinking look – when I urge a boy for example to eat vegetables – to prepare himself to do something not quite pleasant or inviting when especially I know that in his heart of hearts that he knows quite well that it is good and right for him to follow my wishes. Surely you cannot help recognising that the same law 'Be strong and work' applies to the faculties of your brains as much as your physical prowess.

Perhaps only a Headmaster could associate the eating of vegetables with an Old Testament injunction, but it is easy to see what impressed Siegfried so much, the same Thomas Arnold stress on the direction of the faculties, body and mind. Siegfried, in fact, was so taken by the sermon that he wrote down every word of it, sent the copy home to his parents to inwardly digest, and followed it up with a second letter explaining how proud he was of the school for the moral demands it made on the boys. When the Professor sat down to read the sermon, he was no doubt quick to spot the verbal nuances. He had spoken of Siegfried's *needs*; the Headmaster had spoken about Siegfried's *duty*. There, in a nutshell, lay the difference between Arnold and Froebel.

Siegfried moved up the ladder of status and authority at Boxgrove to become a prefect during his final year at the school. It was an early sign of the leadership qualities that would later single him out. He knew well in advance that senior school would mean a move back to Manchester and living at home.

Siegfried entered Manchester Grammar School in the September of 1906, shortly after having reached his fifteenth birthday. He did not stay there very long, leaving as a day-boy in the spring term of 1908. At Boxgrove he had finished top of the pile as a prefect, but at Manchester Grammar things were more daunting, the other boys looking frighteningly tall and the intimidating prefects wearing mortarboards as a sign of their office.

The big jump, of course, was from a junior school to a senior one, but in practice the shift was not as marked as it might first appear. The fact that Boxgrove House and Manchester Grammar had two fundamental charac-teristics in common underlined a sense of continuity.

The first of the characteristics was that each school was firmly aca-demically orientated. Manchester Grammar, founded in 1515, was the older and more prestigious of the two, but it shared with Boxgrove a fervent pursuit of academic excellence. Manchester Grammar was a striking instance of the old, endowed grammar school, often cited as a notable example of academic excellence, so much so that it has been dubbed 'a factory for mass-producing university scholars'. Siegfried would have been no stranger to the hothouse atmosphere he met there.

Then again, Manchester Grammar, no less than Boxgrove, was quick to exhort its alumni to 'Be strong and quit you like Men'. This was such a feature of the school that it even included the notion in the school song 'Hugh of the Owl' :

> Round us are factory, forge and store,
> Market and cattle pen,
> But here in our factory 'mid the roar,
> Work we at making men.

The school's historians noted how it was the 'inspired doggerel of tradition, but in those days boys were sentimental enough to mean it'.[6] The staff of the school certainly meant it. The school was at the hub of a city founded upon and driven by industry; it was indeed surrounded by factory and forge. The rapidly emerging technology called for a new type of 'Men', a new type of leader of the highest calibre, technologically-minded leaders capable of masterminding a modernising industry. There were still plenty of Mancunians on hand to mutter 'where there's muck, there's brass', but the signs were that technology was moving on and unless the right people were in the right place, there would be sufficient muck but not so much brass. Manchester Grammar was in the job of making the 'Men'.

Changes were demanded if the school was going to rise to the challenge. No-one understood this better than Siegfried's High Master, the formidable John Lewis Paton, an authoritarian of the front rank, who took over the school at a time when it was content to rest on its laurels and who injected a fresh sense of purpose into it. It was he who urged masters and boys alike 'to build on all which is pure, manly, noble, and of good report'. The school was rooted in the old classical curriculum and it was Paton who built up the Modern and Mathematics side. Mathematics had always been taught well, with some of the school's outstanding successes being in that field, and by the time Siegfried entered, Paton's reforms had just begun to bite. Paton once wrote: 'The way we spend our leisure is really a test of our education'.[7] Siegfried soon found a plentiful supply of cultural societies he could join. The school was also active in the outdoors. Standing camps at Alderley and in the Lake District were always popular with the boys. The first of the well-known School Treks occurred in 1902. Siegfried did not take part in any of this; he had other fish to fry.

In several respects Siegfried blossomed in the sparkling intellectual environs of the school: it brought a sharper edge to his mind, more polish at the academic level. It looked as if all was going well for him. But on the evidence of the Professor this was far from the case; according to him the

Top: *Siegfried, bottom right, anticipating modern top-roping at the*
   Hermann Lietz-Schule
Foot: *Siegfried in the fire-gutted ruin of the Hermann Lietz-Schule*

special needs still rankled. This time the big difference was that puberty was behind him, he had entered the melancholia of the mid-teens, and it had all to be done at home. The brunt of his silences and fleeting tantrums fell on his parents. It was too much to take. The problem was once again acute enough to dictate a further move, for the tension at home was such that something had to be done, and when the act came it was radical. He would find himself once more a boarder, not on the leafy Surrey downs, but far away in Germany; unexpectedly perhaps Siegfried was to end his schooldays in his mother's country. The definitive and fashioning period of his education was about to begin.

For his final school, Siegfried joined the Hermann Lietz-Schule at Schloss Bieberstein.

Hermann Lietz was the founder of three schools, one at Haubina, a second at Ilsenberg, and the one Siegfried attended at Bieberstein: each establishment operated under the identical system. Schloss Bieberstein was beautifully situated 1600 feet above sea level within sight of the gentle Röhn mountains of the Hesse-spa country. The nearest town of any size was Fulda, well known for its baroque architecture, and on the river of that name. Siegfried boarded in Germany from the May of 1908 to the summer term of 1909

It was at Bieberstein that Siegfried met one of the two men who were to have a seminal influence on the direction of his life. Hermann Lietz was a striking character, powerful and charismatic, with a lively capacity for arousing enthusiasm and discipleship. Siegfried, who became a disciple himself, crystallizing aspects of Lietz's thought into his own, described him as:

> Somewhat short and dark, and looks hardened by a rough life. He has black hair and a moustache. His voice is husky and not loud and I never can understand what he says when he speaks from some way off – nor can anybody else.

When he did speak, he was listened to. Lietz was a visionary, brilliant and autocratic, with an influence on German education which spread well beyond the walls of his own schools. He both took from the British public school and gave back; he learnt from Cecil Reddie at Abbotsholme School and in his turn greatly influenced Kurt Hahn. Siegfried, by finding himself under Lietz, was caught up in the first of a number of precursory or pioneering movements that have since become beacons of the Establishment, in this instance Gordonstoun School.

No two educationalists could be farther apart than Froebel and Lietz. Froebel saw education as a means of changing the individual; Lietz aimed to change society. His education was about an etherealised vision, a vision of a pan-Germanism, a national renewal through the rediscovery of spiritual values. Order was a key word in his vocabulary. He was fearful that the new power released by modern technology posed a threat to order in society. This could be seen in the alienation of the labouring class, the industrial proletariat, common in Siegfried's Manchester as it was throughout the industrial cities of Germany. The unrest represented a serious threat to the cohesion of society, the nation, and he urged a firm restoration of order based upon spiritual values.

Spiritual renewal called for right leadership at the top. He contended that all societies are run from the top down. He openly defended his school as a benevolent élitism. 'Be strong and quit you like Men' might well have been his motto. When he accepted a boy at his school, he looked just as much for leadership potential as for all-round ability; if he did not find those qualities, he did not take the boy. Boys under him found the moral imperatives of duty made so starkly clear that moral virtue became confounded with civic virtue. The boys at his schools were there to be educated so as to oversee society, to direct society and care for it, and to that end a Spartan regime aimed at academic excellence coupled with moral integrity. His inspiration was Plato. A copy of the *Republic* was never far away, and at the slightest provocation, his husky voice blunting the rhythm of the Greek, he would explicate in tones that would both 'instruct and chastise'. His concept of an élite officer class corresponded to Plato's Guardian:

> Then he who is to be a good and noble Guardian of our city will be by nature philosophical and spirited, and quick and strong. *Republic: Book 1*

Lietz adopted Plato's hierarchical notion of education. The upper level of education was reserved for the Guardian class and a lower level for the ordinary citizen. Both levels of education were imperative for the right ordering of the 'city state'. The ordinary citizen had to be educated to conform to the same views on all matters of ethics and politics as those held by the Guardians who framed the laws and laid down the mechanisms of order; the ordinary citizen had also to be educated to occupy the function he or she performed in the community under the leadership of the Guardian. Using these terms of reference, Lietz's schools handled the budding Guardians, but in his view a breakdown had occurred in the education of the ordinary German citizen. The signs were clear with the threat of a revolution in the air. A tottering social order would not suffice to keep at bay two antagonistic classes facing each other in hostile camps as a struggle around industrial production took shape. Patrician and plebeian were at odds as working people, Plato's citizens, questioned their place in society and increasingly challenged the laws and institutions which held them in check. It was against this background of conflict that Lietz turned to education for the spiritual renewal of Germany. So convinced was he, and not without reason, that violence was about to break out that he instituted compulsory officer cadet training in each of his schools. This would be the first taste of military training Siegfried experienced. He might have expected to face officer cadet training at Manchester Grammar, but in fact he missed it by being too early, an Officer Training Corps not having been set up until 1910, well after he left the school. It would be interesting to know whether May, as a classicist herself, held any strong view about officer training being a legitimate extension of the Guardian Ideal or whether brother or sister ever discussed the issue between themselves. The topic was there for the picking. Siegfried came to identify with Lietz's Guardian, enthusiastically endorsed the officer cadet training, and adopted the same line when he left Germany.

On May 3rd, 1908, Siegfried set sail for Lietz's latter-day Republic at Bieberstein in a mood of adolescent adventurousness. It was his first foreign trip on his own and he revelled at the prospect. He savoured every detail; the hubbub at the station; sorting out German train timetables; a conversation with an American lady in the same carriage. He stopped off at Halle, supposedly to stay one night with a relative, but he enjoyed himself so much that he remained on for a second and was subsequently told off in a letter from his parents for doing so. He found the scenery south of Halle so attractive that he said it made him feel 'paintbrushy'. But it was, unfortunately, a thoroughly miserable wet day when he finally reached Fulda. He was not impressed:

> When I got to Fulda, it began to drizzle, but as I had 2 hours to wait, I ventured out into the town, which struck me as decidedly uninteresting. I walked about in some gardens in the pouring rain, till it was time to return.

Back at the station, where the train was waiting to take him to Bieberstein, he quickly fell in with other boys. He was in for a cultural shock when he saw how the boys were dressed:

> I waited a bit about the station looking with suspicion upon all school boys with short trousers. I then entered my train and found myself in the same compartment with a boy with short trousers.

After some time, he asked me if I was going to Bieberstein, and the school. It turned out he was also, although not a new boy. His name was Halbig and he was said to be a very good violinist.

He had obviously not expected that boys at his new school would wear short trousers. It was not so much a jolt to his teenage self-image, as to his Englishness, where boys of his background expected to dress in a jacket and stiff collar, knickerbockers, and long socks down from the knees. He would now be required to dress as a German boy, formal on formal occasions but more relaxed and open otherwise, the start of a change of attitude to dress by him that would become especially noticeable when he was active in the outdoors.

Siegfried was to be given a dramatic opportunity to show what he was made of almost as soon as he reached the school.

One of Lietz's innovations was to introduce the *Gartenban*, a regular weekly session working in the garden, something each boy had to undertake. Siegfried would have every reason to remember his first *Gartenban*. Just as he was about to start, one of the other boys raised the alarm; black smoke was pouring from the roof of the main school building. They rushed over for the start of what turned out to be a long, arduous, and a distinctly dangerous struggle to save the school from burning itself out.

Siegfried's account of the fire is one of the longest pieces in the Braunholtz collection and quite understandably the event left a deep impression on him. It was undoubtedly the most genuinely threatening situation he had to confront in his young life and the way he conducted himself is highly enlightening.

By the time Siegfried and his companions reached the main building all the upstairs rooms were already blazing fiercely. Fortunately for him, Siegfried's room was on the floor below the blaze, which gave him the opportunity to rescue his trunk and belongings. Having successfully got his gear out to a safe place, he turned his attention to Doctor Lietz's library, stocked as it was with important volumes, and after a frantic effort he managed to salvage the most valuable of the items. Then he had to get out – and quickly:

> It was all up with the top storey. Then bare to the waist we proceeded to drag out all the furniture. By this time the inner court was black as night and it was raining, not cats and dogs, but tiles and slates. Whenever we crossed the zone of fire we had to put mattresses on our heads and more than once I caught a tile.

There is a nice touch of boyish bravado about 'and more then once I caught a tile'. But it was not all bravado. He was compelled to take charge in the Chapel when the legs of the grand piano refused to screw off. In the resulting mêlée a number of boys 'lost their heads' as he put it, and he had to stop them adding to the danger by throwing items out of the window onto people below. Siegfried continued:

> We then had to work at carrying water for the fire engines which had arrived. The firemen were just what you would imagine of country people. They walked about outside in their shining helmets, and stood in groups discussing the aspect. When Wander suggested they might attend to the fire, they shook their heads, and said it was too dangerous. They managed to fix up a hose outside however. This drew water from a bath which had to be continually filled with buckets of water carried from the wash cellar. We therefore made a chain by which the full buckets were passed along hand to hand on one line, and returned along another. I happened to stand just by the door where bits of slate etc. were continually falling, and had to keep one eye fixed upon the roof above and the other on the man on my right. However, nothing happened. After we had eaten some bread and sausage, we then went into the court, for by now the top storey with the roof and all the rest was completely gone. But in many parts the storey below was blazing. The firemen were afraid to ascend the ladders and pour water on the flames, and so Wander took the hose out of their hands and worked while they looked on. The Kapelle and Speisesaal, the former next to my room, were chiefly in flames, and before long the Speisesaal, at least the roof, came thundering down. Then some of us worked at pouring water on the blazing Kapelle, and we had just retreated for more water when there was a big crash and the roof came in. After that my chief occupation was watching the roof of a room quite below where the roof threatened to come in from the 2nd storey, and which was important because it was the key to the Laboratorium, and other important rooms. Every time a bit of roof came in, water had to be poured on it. I was at this about four hours in all. At 1 in the morning we had some coffee which we much needed. It tasted delicious, although they assured me that it was 'Schenslick'. I found out afterwards that a good many of the fellows had gone down to sleep at Langenbieber in the Hotel. But I and a few others determined to keep on till the firemen came a bit to their senses. During the night a large number of witnesses came up to the castle to seek

plunder, and in the lower area where things were being stored one could often see a suspicious looking person walking about, and when one asked what they wanted they said they were looking for some things belonging to their sister who was a servant at the castle. Later on I helped in receiving various things which the peasants were bringing down into Langenbieber. This was the most trying part as the people all wanted to talk to you and ask what such and such an instrument was for, and when they discovered I was English they wanted to know all about England.

The fire had been a test of nerve and stamina and Siegfried had acquitted himself brilliantly. Bare to the waist, lathered in grime, he had led from the front. John Laycock wrote of him: 'He almost always led because it was his right'.[8] That right began to earn its spurs during the fire. The blaze, for him, was a confirmation of Lietz's doctrine of the Guardian, for 'what you might imagine of country people' manifestly called for leadership, direction and discipline from the boy named Wander and himself. He was utterly scathing about the firemen. His disdain shows through and he was determined to stay at his post 'till the firemen came a bit to their senses'. It was his job to see that they did. He was just as equally dismissive of the 'peasants' either marauding about the castle or lugging things down to Langenbieber, supervising and checking what they did, condescendingly weary of their infernal questions. He owed little loyalty to the school, having only been at it a few days, but when the crisis came he acquitted himself like a man, doing his 'duty' in a manner that would have made his old Boxgrove headmaster proud. He tells us that after the drama was over he slept a solid nine hours and awoke feeling like 'a new man'. The building had been far too badly damaged for masters or boys to stay on. Siegfried was taken to Lietz's other school at Haubina, where he stayed for five months, following exactly the same regime he would have done had he remained at Bieberstein. It was one further school to add to the list.

By the summer of 1909, Siegfried's schooldays effectively came to an end, but he was not yet done with Lietz or Lietz with him. The adventurous way he spent the school holiday again shows him participating in what has now become commonplace in schools but which, at the time, was thoroughly pioneering. He took part in a Lietz-Schule expedition abroad. It is on record that his parents were strongly against his going, but he deployed the opportunity-not-to-be-lost card with masterful cunning, and they relented. Siegfried was off to Iceland.

It is sad to report that knowledge of the Iceland expedition is disappointingly scanty, particularly in the light of its adventurous nature, and the modern feel about the project. If Siegfried's personal diary of the expedition exists, it has not been found, which obviously leaves us with a gap. The gap has to some extent been filled by Herr Ulrich Kindscher, of the Hermann Lietz-Schule, who succeeded in unearthing an account written for the school magazine. *Von der Islandreise* under the initials St-L.W., is a popular version of events slanted to catch the interest of the schoolboy reader, although the bold outline gives us some idea of what took place.

The party consisted of two masters and ten boys. At Reykjavik they engaged two guides, both students, and it has to be said that their competency is open to some doubt.

It took three days to sail from Copenhagen to Reykjavik by way of Leith. Reykjavik, now a modern city, then still retained the air of a frontier town, permeated with a faint sulphurous smell from the geothermally heated water, and with ponies and pigs running at will through the streets. Still, the place was well organised, and the party had no problem getting the ponies they wanted and the bulk of their supplies. From Reykjavik a chartered motorboat took them to a wild sandy spit, two hours from the nearest hamlet, near the foot of the 4,000 foot high Eyjafjajokull.

The first part of the expedition gave each boy the chance to tackle the objective of his choice. The school magazine limits itself to saying that one party climbed the Hekla. That Siegfried was one of the boys is confirmed by a picture postcard of the Hekla he sent home, marked up with the date of the climb, July 21st, and also marked with the names of the boys who made the ascent with him. The Hekla was a realistic choice. Siegfried did the first part of the trek by pony, then, leaving the pony behind, he had to cross a rough lava stretch before taking an easy snow route to the rim of the volcano's crater. The cone-shaped Hekla, at 4892 feet, does not constitute one of the 'great' mountains, but in 1909 there would not have been many boys of eighteen with it on his list of completed peaks.

For the second part of the expedition the boys split into a senior and junior group. Under the supervision of a guide, and with one master, the five younger boys undertook a six-day trek of their own. The older lads, meanwhile, were to traverse the Langjokull, and then on the sixth day the entire party would rendezvous, walking back out together. Siegfried was in the traversing party.

The Langjokull, 70-kilometres long and 30-kilometres wide, angled more or less S.W. to N.E., is typical of the rough Icelandic interior, making up a glistening white plateau with ribs of ice that ooze down folded blanched cirques. It is a wilderness with all the solemnity and solitude of the high mountains. The only way Siegfried's group could get onto it involved a painful slog. First, there was a brown-black lava field, a messy surface to walk on, with the necessity of regularly clearing chips of grit that had seeped into the boots. This was followed by fording bitterly cold glacial streams eddying down silted troughs. These streams, often obstructed by polished boulders, were tricky to tackle with heavy loads, having to be crossed by adopting a ferry-glide technique.

Once on the plateau, the party improvised a sledge out of ski-poles, intending to manhaul their equipment and food in the best Captain Scott style. Oddly, the equipment did not include tents. At night they stuffed their individual sleeping-bags into a large corporate covering, hardly a satisfactory arrangement, but it at least had the virtue of providing the sledge loads with protection during the day. The boys quickly discovered how bone-racking manhauling a sledge can be. On the ups and downs of disfigured terrain, and in the swish and swash of melt-snow, the sledge is forever twisting and pulling awkwardly out of line. Chaffed limbs, cuts, and hand blisters resulted as they were bound to do.

Day five turned out to be the bad day – the danger day. An extremely tired party woke up to find a wretchedly cold mist had clamped down over the plateau. It was exactly the type of weather condition that can so easily catch out a tired party. The account in the school magazine is not clear about whether there was a blunder in navigation, which sounds the most likely, or whether the map misled the party, but either way they found themselves hopelessly off course. As always, there was a price to pay. First they

Postcard of Hekla marked by Siegfried with the names of his companions

had to get themselves into, and afterwards out of, a savagely deep V-shaped trough. The flanks of the trough consisted of smooth ice, and while they could feel the cold air wafting up from below, the mist made it impossible for them to see the bottom. It was at this point that they set about a near-lethal manoeuvre. Fatigue had taken its toll and they were so anxious to make progress that they cast all caution aside by sliding the sledge with everything on it on a free run down the ice flank and then glissaded after it themselves. This brings the judgment of the guide and master in charge into serious question. The golden rule of glissading is never to start off unless there is a perfectly clear view of what lies beneath. How were they to know what laid below? Supposing the mist had hidden a crevasse just waiting to swallow up the sledge. An exhausted party would have found themselves stranded without food or sleeping-bags, even supposing they had escaped unharmed. The gods of Balder and Thor were on their side, however, and they got away with it. The gods turned out to be even kinder when they pulled themselves up to the rim of the trough on the further side, when suddenly the mist cleared and revealed a breathtaking vista in the dream-glow of the midnight sun, a kaleidoscope of brilliant northland colours against the white of the snow. Life came trickling back as the evening held the sun, and after 29 hours of slogging over the plateau on a paltry slice of bread, the boys were content to sit and stare. Siegfried, to coin a phrase, had taken part in an epic.

The rendezvous with a worried junior party was now a day behind schedule. There was an urgent need to keep pushing on if they were to catch the boat for home. After the link had been successfully made, the combined party set out on a forced march, a hard slog which they accomplished by dividing walking into 4 hour spells interlaced with an hour's break. Taking into account the rough terrain they had to cover, it was no small achievement on its own.

At Leith, in Scotland, on the return, Siegfried said his farewells to the boys who had climbed the Hekla with him and shared the long sweat of the plateau traverse. They had to board a second boat that would take them home to Denmark before catching a train which would finally land them home in Germany. Siegfried travelled south back to Manchester on his own.

The long train journey gave Siegfried plenty of time to ponder and reflect on all that had happened to him during the tangled web of a convoluted school career. He must have felt with some justice that he had already travelled a long distance between Lady Barn House and the Hermann Lietz-Schule. Outwardly it looked as if the schools belonged to two irreconcilable worlds. There was little or nothing in common between Froebel's inner law of Divine Unity and Lietz's vision of the Guardian Ideal. Each school had been talking a different language and telling him opposite things. Yet it seems that is not the way Siegfried himself heard what had been said. Both schools had laid down terms of reference, and far from feeling cut in half, he viewed himself as the axis of the dynamic interplay between polar opposites. He had made a break that is for sure, but behind the break he retained the continuity of a line of values. The child-centred Lady Barn House, with its passion-driven care and concern for the individual inner law, represented the quintessence of his family's liberal values, and these were never going to leave him. What he had done was to reject their libertarian mode of expression. He looked for a way of putting old wine into new bottles. He had gravitated away from the efficacy of libertarian structures in favour of Lietz's tough concepts of discipline and responsibility and order. He was intuitively predisposed to Lietz's stress on the importance of order by virtue of his own experience of inner disorder. His early failure to control and direct his faculties of mind and body, had wreaked havoc on himself, set up tensions between himself and his parents, and patently ruined his dealings with Lady Barn House. The Guardian Ideal offered him the structure to reinterpret how he felt he had to express his own personal concern for the welfare of the individual and society. This would have implications later on, both in the manner in which he conducted himself and also in how he came to view what had to be done in an increasingly technological age. He was not yet finished with the injunction, 'Be strong and quit you like Men', which had so impressed him in a sermon he had copied out in full.

Siegfried returned home in buoyant mood and the Professor made a special point of saying how much more mature he appeared to be. He was ready to move forward and take on university. And by now, out there, the beckoning mountains were waiting.

CHAPTER FOUR

BICYCLING

The sketch of Siegfried's childhood at Aberystwyth, and the outline of his school career, contains little reference to outdoor activity other than the expedition to Iceland. It should not be assumed from this that nothing had taken place. There never had been a time when mountains or any other type of outdoor activity had not played a central part in his life. 'He looks radiant', the Professor wrote to Marie Herford in the April of 1906, 'and the boys ask him, he says, if he has been to the Sahara'. One of the things that had given him a worthy tan was the frequent use of his bicycle.

It is perhaps a surprise to discover that not only Siegfried, but the Herford entourage, including his mother, were bicycling addicts. The biggest surprise of all is to find the Professor at it, particularly in the light of his asthma, but if anything he proved the biggest addict of them all. Every Easter holiday he would take himself off for a week or ten days, carefully planning each tour, his head stuffed with the sixteenth century and his pockets with paintbrush and sketch pad. These tours seem to have been the highlight of his year.

The keenness for the bicycle may come as less of a surprise when we recall that Siegfried had an uncle who was a key player in the growing bicycle industry. It is a striking example of how the Herford family's Manchester Unitarian network smoothed Siegfried's path for him. All he had to do was to take tea with a devoted aunt, Mary Renold, née Mary Susan Herford, a lady always to be found on a Sunday morning in her pew at Cross Street Unitarian Chapel. She had married Hans Renold in 1880, a native of Aarau in Switzerland, an engineer of great ability and imagination. Hans Renold possessed the sort of drive that got things done. His prospective father-in-law lent him £300 to buy out the small textile chains business of James Slater, and he never looked back; his brilliant inventiveness led to a successful business. James Slater had already obtained the first British driving chains patent in 1864, a patent Hans Renold took over, and in the year of his marriage he patented the bush roller (bicycle) chain and followed this up five years later by inventing the silent inverted tooth chain. It was the type of creative engineering that instinctively appealed to Siegfried and he became a frequent visitor to his uncle's factory, Renolds Chains.

Renolds Chains prospered on the strength of an expanding market. Bicycling had got off to a successful start in Victorian times, and although the Cycle Touring Club had been founded in 1878, it was not until machines were built with two low wheels in the 'nineties that the big explosion came about. The bicycle, so cheap and convenient, turned out to prove a great liberator for thousands of ordinary people, an aspect of the invention which on its own delighted the Herfords. By the time Siegfried was active, groups of young bicyclists could be found out and about on any average Sunday, strung along the country lanes, excitingly exploring the countryside for themselves. These Sunday outings became so popular that the railways competed for custom by laying on cheap-day tickets. Mostly in use was a solid-looking 'breaker' with a wicker basket attached to the handlebar.

A search of the Cycle Touring Clubs' archives showed that none of the Herfords ever joined. There could well have been a political explanation behind this. The Herfords, keen Liberals as they were, would have been aware that in the north of England the Cycle Touring Club had forged close ties with the Labour movement. That would not have gone down at all well.

We are lucky to possess two quite full accounts of bicycle tours that involve Siegfried. One took place in Germany. But first there is the Professor's Easter tour of North Wales in the April of 1907, unusual in that he took Siegfried with him, and notable because it marked Siegfried's first ascent of Snowdon. The chronicle is based on a series of letters the Professor wrote to Marie Herford at the end of each day telling her where they were and what they had done. The letters convey a wonderfully evocative feel of what Snowdonia was like in those far-off days.[1]

Father and son left Manchester on April 3rd. The aim on the first day was to reach the Wynnstay Arms Hotel at Ruthin. There was to be no rush, with plenty of stops *en route*, a chance to visit various places of artistic or historical interest. But it did not go well. The places visited might have been of absorbing interest to the Professor, but which 'Siegfried could hardly be got to look at', being frustrated by the delays. Siegfried just wanted to get on with it and leave art and history alone.

Nor did things improve once they arrived at the Wynnstay Arms Hotel, the Professor recording a wretched attack of asthma:

> S meanwhile is a capital fellow and I am sorry that I have to put his qualities to the test in one respect, by having asthma last night. He is always very loving and tender to me when I am in any sort of suffering, more almost than May; and tho' I generally prefer to have asthma alone, or only with thee, I could not regret his presence.

It is a highly revealing comment about the relationship between father and son. Still, Siegfried gained ample compensation for his ministrations, for the food at the Hotel was excellent, and he enjoyed a huge breakfast almost on a par with the even vaster meal of the night before, one of several references to just how much Siegfried tucked away to the astonishment of his father.

Despite the asthmatic disturbances of the night, they were away reasonably early, and reached Pentrefoelas:

> S. found much satisfaction in a grand ravine where the road winds up at one point, and photographed the bridge. He has been using films at a great rate – 10 of the set altogether; but has had some good subjects. Of course Snowdon was the great feast. We have really been in luck, and I am glad he has had the long deferred satisfaction at last. It was a fresh clear morning, not too bright, but the peaks as we rode down to Bettws - 7 miles, thro' a wooden glen, downhill all the way, stood out in lovely opalescent blues and purples, delicately outlined against the sky; some of the peaks of Snowdon visible behind Moel Siabod, were towering in front - the nearest to the Greek mountains. At Bettws we bought some biscuits and chocolate, and a MG, and started up the road for Pen-y-Gwyryd: I had some difficulty in persuading S. to stop at the Swallow Falls. What was a waterfall, when Snowdon was coming? However he went and took a photograph of it. Then on to Capel Curig, where the first clear view burst upon us – the whole group, from Llwydd (sic) to Crib Goch, and the great peak in the middle, all day and perfectly cloudless and clear. At Gorphwysfa, a few min. past 12.30., we deposited out bicycles (taking off our waterproofs to carry, observe O Prudent Mother!) and set off.

The two of them had arrived at the top of the Llanberis Pass, dominated on one side by the hoary rocks of Crib Goch, with on the other the sweep of the Glyders. Below lay the drop of the rugged valley with its cliffs which look as if they will close in and crush Gorphwyspha, the old hotel, with 'its bed and its brass': once described by the irascible John Tyndall as a 'small public house'. It was very much a gathering point for climbers but has since been metamorphosed into an enlarged and ugly youth hostel. Opposite the hotel in those days stood a rusty shack, the Welsh headquarters of Oscar Eckenstein, a German engineer with a huge safari beard, an expert on balance technique who made the first ascent of Lliwedd's Central Gully.

The two of them set off along the Miner's Track, contouring the rim of

Cwm Dyli, and they could see *en face* the impressively intricate precipice of Lliwedd beyond the dark waters of Llydaw. This was not the first time they had stood together in the great hollow. In 1903 they had shared an attempt to climb Snowdon, but had been compelled to retreat when they were reasonably high, having run into bad weather:

It was interesting to notice all the points of our unlucky expedition 3 years ago – like the heroes of an Arctic exploring ship, marking the spots where some hapless predecessor had left his bones, or where his umbrella had broken, or his hat blown off. Altho' so much more auspicious than that occasion, we agreed it was not so grand; the awful bleakness of the mountain hollow under the cloud, which we were exploring to its inmost fastnesses, incurring the fury of all his winds and waters – was more impressive than the beautiful unmysterious clearness of today, with every peak clear – save for a flake of woolly cloud now and then, and hardly a breath stirring, even on top. We noticed where we had then to turn back: a pretty good way below the edge of the ravine, you may like to know. S. had a scramble up the steep part, while I preferred the zigzag made by the regular path (there was nothing in the least dangerous, only rough). We stopped diverse times, I think he took 6 of Snowdon altogether; one of Llwydd's peaks, with me in the foreground; one of Crib Goch with *him* in the foreground; one of the top from Llyn Llydaw, another from the path above Llyn Glas, and so on.[2] He thoroughly enjoyed himself, as you may suppose. The only distraction was, that on reaching the ridge, we found the view beyond all hidden in cloud – the clouds as it were driving against the N and W faces of the mountain and there resting, for the S and E faces were perfectly clear as I said – save for little puffs of vapour that now and then pushed forward over the edge, like little supernumerary imps thrusting themselves on the stage before their turn comes to play. However, before we left, the cloud veil had partly lifted, and we saw at least dimly the lake towards Caernarvon, and the sea, with the Glyders and Carnedds. S. was keen in his regrets for the deprival of the wide prospect to the north: I reminded him that 3 years ago he had scorned the idea of the view being of any importance if only he reached the top. He has got a little beyond that now, and largely I think thro' photography. We had some tea up there; but the top is sadly spoiled by the hotels and the railway; and not only that but the beautiful sharpness of the peak is positively damaged from many views by the hotels, which are placed on the very summit, and make a perceptively blunt finale. After staying half an hour, we started down, having not very much superfluous daylight, as we meant to ride to Beddgelert. About 6 we reached Gorphwysfa, and it was a delightful change after rough walking over stones, which left our feet rather sore, to mount our steel horses and sail down Gwynant ...

At Beddgelert they had booked into the Temperance Hotel, where the evening meal was served late, much to the hungry Siegfried's disgust. But it had been a memorable day: he had scaled Snowdon for the first time by the Miner's Track, as many a young beginner has done before him and since. It was not to be by any means the last Snowdon would hear of him.

The Professor's power of endurance and stamina had been remarkable. Despite an attack of asthma during the night at Ruthin, he had ridden all the distance from there to Snowdon, took himself up and down the peak, then peddled down to Beddgelert where that same evening he still had sufficient energy left to pen a 700-word letter to his wife. Siegfried's own legendary powers of endurance had a good pedigree. It was small wonder that on the following day, April 5th, they intended to take life easy, although the plan was to reach Dolgellau that evening.

The morning of the 5th they spent lingering on a farm at Blaen Namor, under the shapely Cnicht, where the Professor and Marie Herford had spent holidays together before the children were born. Their reward was a superb vista of the Snowdon massif: 'exquisite in its opalescent shimmer of delicate gold and greys and amethyst and pink and orange'. (Had Siegfried been clairvoyant, he might have sensed the poignancy about where he now found himself, a little above Hafod Owen, the cypher of trees where the ashes of the darkly troubled Menlove Edwards now lie scattered in full sight of the same vista. But it was not a moment for thoughts of lost content.) As the Professor read, Siegfried used the time to explore the area and take a swim. It was all delightfully tempting and as a consequence they dallied too long. They failed to take account of the wind, how strongly it had risen, and finding themselves riding against it, they took 4·5 hours to cover the 30 miles to Dolgellau.

As the tour drew to a comfortable close, the Professor found himself captivated by the moody charm of the variegated lower hills of the Border country. He fell in love with Clun, assuring his wife that correctly the name rhymed with *sun*, and he delayed long enough to complete a number of paintings that are still safely preserved. In two vital respects the tour had proved a success. The weather, by and large, had been good for an Easter and the planned route was completed. More fundamentally, father and son had got on well together.

The German Tour June 1908. The second bicycling expedition took place in Germany. It was integral to Hermann Lietz's approach to social education that his pupils undertook a journey of some kind. In this instance the journey took place fairly quickly after the fire at Bieberstein; in fact before Siegfried had been installed at the alternative school in Haubina – an indication perhaps that until the situation was sorted out, it relieved the pressure to pack off some of the older boys for a while.

At the time, the idea of young people's expeditions had very much integrated itself into the *Jugenkultur,* due to the success of the nationwide youth movement known as the *Wandervogel.* The *Wandervogel* had been founded in the year Siegfried moved into Didsbury, 1901, the work of Hermann Holmann, a youth leader of genius. Holmann had started the *Wandervogel* in an endeavour to counteract the nihilistic attitude, arising from the poverty and lack of employment, and the bad health of so many young people restlessly surviving in the big industrial cities. He set up cheaply-run expeditions into the countryside as an antidote to the threateningly depressing social scene:

> Youth had to rediscover nature, the fields, woods, brooks, lakes, and meadows from which the city dweller had been alienated.[3]

The aim of the *Wandervogel* was to encourage self-education through self -reliance and shared group activities. A popular focal point for expeditions was the Harz mountains, and it was there that Holmann first established a series of cheap, self-catering bunkhouses or hostels – *Landheime* – an idea that spread right across Germany (In 1930, when the Youth Hostels Association was formed, the *Landheime* were used as a prototype). Siegfried's school expedition fitted into the Wandervogel mould without actually belonging to it. Lietz backed the Wandervogel as an extension of his campaign for spiritual renewal through education: it took the campaign beyond the confines of the Guardian to the ordinary citizen in the shape of working – or non-working – young people.

The tour of North Wales the previous year had provided Siegfried with useful tips he could build on. He had learnt a bit more about how to plan an expedition, the value of carefully pacing yourself, and if the expedition was by bicycle, take into account the wind factor. Knowing is one thing, however, and application another. In this instance the expedition turned out to be one of those innocently youthful enterprises when one can hardly be said to have camped unless the tent gets blown down and it was destined for an abrupt end.

On June 14th, 1908, Siegfried sent home to his parents what he called 'a gigantic' eight-page letter, describing in graphic detail an account of the expedition. The basic facts are that the party consisted of six boys under the leadership of a lad named Kömer; there was no accompanying member of staff; the boys slept in cheap hotels, even cheaper inns, or sometimes in the forest woods where they cooked their own meals on an open fire. They had been told to wear their red school caps, and with a typical teenager's regard for image, he noted how this caused a stir in each village they passed through.

The party adopted an eight-day circular route, taking in Bamburg, followed by the more southerly Munich, then veering northwards again to the medieval Rothenburg.

When the party arrived at Regensburg they stopped on the magnificent Steinerne Brücke over the Danube, where Siegfried, perhaps under the influence of his father's Norse mythology, had persuaded his companions to divert to the Valhalla, named after the place where the Valkyries brought the slain heroes of battle, but at Regensburg a museum stuffed with grotesque objects and known as the Hall of Fame:

> Which stands on a wooded hill overlooking the Danube and behind it are the hills which run along the side of the Dan. It is of the same type as the Parthenon of Athens.

The keenness to see the Valhalla marked a radical change in Siegfried since the Easter tour of North Wales. Then, on the stretch between Manchester and Ruthin, the Professor gave up trying to get Siegfried to show even a glimmer of interest in historical or artistic venues he wished to inspect. Now it was an altogether different story; he wanted to see things for himself. It was all part of the same broadening of perspective the Professor had noticed on the summit of Snowdon when Siegfried was anxious for the cloud to clear and reveal the full extent of the view. He was no longer satisfied just to bag a top any more than he was content to reel off mile after mile in Germany without exploring the world about him.

The encouraging signs of a growing maturity were not across the board. Under a boiling sun the party pressed on to Augsburg, where, a couple of miles beyond the city, one of the bikes suffered a puncture. That misfortune proved the least of their worries:

> But then the stupid thing happened. In riding round a steep curve, Kömer fell and sliced his knee, so that we could not go on any more.

Kömer's knee was in a bad shape and it was immediately obvious that boys and bikes would have to finish the expedition by train. This was not as easy as it sounds. 'Boyishly', as Siegfried put it, they had all spread their wings during the early stage of the tour and by the time the accident occurred their financial reserves were at a minimum, leaving them short of the train fare. Siegfried himself was reduced to his last 50 Pfennigs. He told his parents: 'And thus it is that I am left with a deficit of 7 – 8 marks.'

He was not to be the first intrepid explorer to find the expedition in debt on its return, although how they managed without the necessary money for the train fare he did not explain. Back at school, when there had been a chance to digest and evaluate the experience, there were lessons to be drawn from an exercise designed to bring them out.

CHAPTER FIVE

A MOUNTAIN LEGACY

Siegfried now entered the era when he began to develop as a mountaineer and climber.

Firstly, a word needs to be said about sources, or more strictly the limited nature of them. A number of Siegfried's later climbs have been well documented, but it is on the earlier years that we find notable gaps. John Laycock wrote: 'He had done a little desultory rock-climbing in England and Wales during 1909 - 1910'.[1] It would be wise not to rely too much on Laycock's words, for there are pointers which suggest that prior to 1909 he had been doing something better than desultory climbing, especially when we take into account his age and the general level of climbing at the time. The most lamentable restriction is the absence of a personal climbing log, for if Siegfried did maintain one it has not been traced. The nearest we get to a list of climbs are the entries he made in his own copy of George Abraham's well-known book *The Complete Mountaineer*, published in 1907 (See Appendix Three), although here again his lists are far from complete. Our knowledge of what he climbed before 1909, or who he climbed with, is an area for further research.

Despite these uncertainties, we can say firmly that Siegfried's contact with mountains began at a very early age. During his Aberystwyth days, as far back at 1895, when he was only four years of age, the Professor took him to the summit of Cader Idris. That is on record. From the summit he gazed for the first time beyond the tangled gullies of the northern edge over to the Snowdon massif pencilled on the horizon, and when later, scrambling the serrated Eastern Arête of Cyfrwy on his own as a teenager, he must have looked back on that revealing moment with relish.

Siegfried's early introduction on Cader Idris would suggest that mountains were in the blood. There is no doubt that his family bequeathed to him a priceless mountain legacy.

To put the legacy into perspective we have to go back to William Henry Herford, and interestingly, in the light of what we already know about the bicycle tour and the visit to Iceland, to the idea of young people's expeditions. The patron saint of all young people's expeditions is the intriguing Rodolphe Topffer, the founder and headmaster of an international school in Geneva, who as early as 1838 led parties of boys on alpine expeditions.

The boys were in good hands, for Topffer was an alpinist of merit, as he needed to be if he was to guide his young parties safely around the Alps at a time when mountaineering proper had barely got a foothold. Topffer, in his turn, influenced Wilhelm von Fellenberg at his Hofwyl Froebelian school. Von Fellenberg took advantage of the good summer weather to lead his young charges over glaciers and high alpine passes.[2] William Henry Herford was quick to latch onto the idea, and when at Lancaster he founded Castle Howell School in 1850, he copied what he had found at Hofwyl and introduced expeditions. While not having the Alps close to hand like von Fellenberg, he did have the Lake District, visible from Lancaster like a distant evocation. When William Henry Herford came to evaluate the importance of the expeditions he did so in holistic terms:

> These annual expeditions lasted but three days; yet parent and teacher will know that their safe adventure, the climbs and walks, boating on the lake, learning to love Nature by examining flowers and observing birds, the comradeship between teacher and pupil, did foster growth and unfolding of body, mind and soul. [3]

One of those to benefit from a Castle Howell expedition was the Professor who had become a pupil at the school in 1862, and found himself in the Lake District that same year. The visit was the foundation of a lifelong passion for The Lakes, a legacy he handed down to his son and daughter.

It might be said that the inheritance came to fruition during the gloriously hot and dry summer of 1903. It was in that year that the family began a series of annual Lake District holidays. These regular visits, notable as an occasion when the family were all together, extended over a period of ten years. They had about them the old thrill of over the hills and far away and lingered endearingly in the memory.

There are two vignettes of Siegfried related to the Lakeland holidays.

The first incident took place in the July of 1906. He had teamed up with his mother for an ascent of Helvellyn. They set out on a morning when the tops and ridges were covered in cloud. They had toiled up the long slope above Thirlmere, and were approaching the summit flank, when all of a sudden the cloud lifted and they had the whole magical view eastwards over Ullswater at their feet. 'O mother', Siegfried burst out, 'can there be anything more beautiful on earth?' It was a rare impromptu outburst, such as he would only risk in the company of his mother, a sign of their close and intimate bond.

The second story shows him in a different light. For this we have to go to the following year, 1907, and it involves a friend of the family and one-time student of the Professor's. Elizabeth Parker was on a walking holiday with two other female companions. Late one afternoon the three ladies unexpectedly spotted Siegfried pounding full tilt down the side of a hill. He had, in fact, been the first to see them. After greetings, he escorted the ladies back to Troutbeck, where they were to join his mother. In a letter to Marie Herford, Elizabeth Parker commented on how struck she had been by Siegfried's action, and she wondered how many other boys of sixteen would have shown such politeness to three older ladies he scarcely knew. But then, when the mood struck him, Siegfried's charm could prove as bewitching as his manners were impeccable.

Elizabeth Parker had stumbled across Siegfried when he was out on his own. Being alone was by no means unusual during family holidays. He used the time in the Lake District to teach himself mountain lore, and was very successful at it, so much so that by the age of fifteen he was perfectly capable of looking after himself (the boy who scaled the Hekla with the Hermann Lietz-Schule was anything but a greenhorn). The solitary outings did not always go down well. His parents often anxiously waited about for him after a long day wandering over the ridges when he did not return until 'the day's last shining bar'.

A story told by the Professor makes it clear that Siegfried was rock-climbing in addition to ridge walking. An incident took place during the summer of 1908, when the family based their holiday on High Nest, near Keswick. The Professor explained what happened after Siegfried had followed his custom of being out all day on his own:

> As night approached, his mother, a little anxious, had gone along the drive to meet him. Presently she saw him coming, and with a face so radiantly happy that she asked what had happened to him. "Something nice", he replied. "I can see that, but what is it?" "Oh nothing much, I have been up Napes Needle, that's all".

It is a charming story, but tantalisingly told, leaving important details unsaid. Questions abound. Had Siegfried walked all the distance from Keswick, climbed Napes Needle, then walked all the way back to High Nest? More important, had he climbed the Needle on his own, in the same manner as the first ascent by W.P. Haskett Smith in 1886? If not, then who had been with him? It would have been exceptional for a boy of seventeen to have tackled the Needle on his own in 1908. Either way, with a companion or not, the incident presupposes a considerable amount of previous rock-climbing practice, pushing Laycock's date back by at least a year, and probably more, for there is a letter from May to her mother saying she had seen Siegfried putting his climbing clothes away in a wardrobe after the 1907 holiday. It is abundantly clear from Siegfried's excited reaction that he knew all about the Needle, and had familiarised himself with the line of ascent, in a way which suggests that he saw it as the realisation of an ambition which he had harboured for quite a long time.

The solitary activity of the family holidays would later give Siegfried a feeling of affinity with Hugh Rose Pope. Throughout his climbing career, despite the fact that he was both selective and exceedingly difficult to get to know, Siegfried nevertheless forged a number of important climbing partnerships and lasting friendships, but as with Hugh Rose Pope, the lure of climbing on his own never left him. He showed every sympathy with Rose Pope when he wrote, 'the climber should sometimes go alone ... let him make his bed in the heather undisturbed by any sign of the presence of man or his handiwork'. [4] By 1912, when the perilous nature of solo climbing was underlined by Rose Pope's death on the Pic du Midi d'Ossau, an isolated peak in the Pyrenees, Siegfried had consciously consolidated what he had intuitively imbibed as a boy. He always held Rose Pope's routes in the highest regard and the South-West on Pillar remained one of his favourite climbs.

The richest legacy Siegfried inherited from William Henry Herford's expeditionary vision was the way that intimacy with the mountain environment came naturally to him. His senses blended with the myriad shapes of the hills, their passing moods and signs, the intricacies of rocky ground. Every fissure came to mean something to him. The slightest movement here or there conveyed a message never left to chance. He felt instinctively at home in the half-light of mists that rolled down to meet him. Perception and discernment went hand in hand so that it was almost as if the mountains passed through him rather than he the mountains. His great-uncle was more true than he knew when he spoke of the unfolding of body, mind and soul. There was an unremitting unfolding of the legacy as the mountains increasingly dominated and directed Siegfried's mind and body.

CLIMBING DAYS

1909 – 1914

To whom the mountain stillness is a song

    More sweet and strong

Than all by human art and rapture poured

    From voice or chord.

An ecstacy that thrills and fires the blood

    Half understood ...

Made them aware that a great mountain, nearer,

    Deeper and clearer,

Into our mystic cadence brings

    The Soul of things.

Of Stillness   C.H. Herford

CHAPTER SIX

MANCHESTER CLIMBER

Siegfried registered as a student at the School of Engineering, University of Manchester, in the autumn of 1909, following his return from Iceland. Entering the School of Engineering was a natural progression for him. Mr Richard Renold, grandson of Hans Renold, the founder of Renolds Chains, has suggested in a letter that Siegfried's interest in engineering might well have been triggered by the many visits he made to the family firm as a boy. As Mr Renold added, he cannot vouch for it, but it seems an eminently reasonable suggestion. Engineering was guaranteed to attract a young man of his practical intellect.

At the School of Engineering, Siegfried found himself under the tutelage of the remarkable Professor J.E.Petavel, one of two men, the other being Hermann Lietz, who exercised a major influence on him at this stage of his life. Petavel was an outstanding pioneer in the field of aeronautics and it was through his encouragement that Siegfried adopted the same path. A pioneer is not too strong a term. Aeronautics in those days stood dubiously on the fringe of engineering, regarded with a mixture of suspicion and amusement, and even at Manchester, engineers of the orthodox variety seriously doubted its value. Siegfried, with a more prophetic view of the future, saw aeronautics as representing an emerging modernity. For those with eyes to see, it was a period heady with prospect. At the very time Siegfried was on the Langjokull icecap with the Hermann Lietz-Schule, Bleriot created a sensation by flying across the Channel, a sure sign of the extent to which an aeroplane could be powered and controlled.

The School of Engineering at the time Siegfried joined it had so few staff or students that everybody knew everybody else. One notable contemporary of his, also under Petavel's wing, was the nineteen-year-old future philosopher Ludwig Wittgenstein. Wittgenstein had arrived at the School of Engineering as a research student a year before Siegfried. His research into aeronautics involved experimenting on the design and construction of box-kites capable of carrying scientific instruments. His biographer described how the bulk of his work was done at the Upper Atmosphere Station, a meteorological observation centre on the outskirts of Glossop, and how when he was there he lived at the isolated Grouse Inn, constantly complaining 'of the incessant rain and the rustic standards of the food and the toilet facilities', although, the more accustomed he grew to it, the better he enjoyed his surroundings.[1] Wittgenstein looked forward to Saturdays when Petavel regularly visited the observation centre with one or two of his students. It was while he was engaged on research at Manchester that he first began to turn to philosophy by way of pure mathematics. There is no direct evidence that the two men met, or engaged in mutual conversation, although had they done so, Siegfried would have relished the meeting of minds. Both young men, in their respective ways, lived life on the edge.

Siegfried was one of the earliest of a long line of Manchester University engineers – he could conceivably even have been the first – who established for themselves an enviable reputation in the climbing world. It was a vastly different world from the wide-open one we are faced with today.

Those who made up the mountaineering and climbing world in Siegfried's day constituted a select group. Behind the capacious Norfolk jackets, the baggy knee-breeches, the spiral puttees and tricouni-nailed boots, could be found the 'Men' Siegfried had first encountered at Boxgrove House School. They were the long-limbed public school 'chaps', the barristers, senior civil–servants, high ranking army officers, school masters and clergymen, for whom cultural distinction and social respectability counted as much as climbing ability. This is not to say that the majority of people visiting the mountain areas in ever increasing numbers belonged to the same group. They did not. The popular mountain areas were having to face a huge increase of holiday tourists drawn from a wide social spectrum. Even by then, the holiday rush was on; *The Field* magazine for March 1913 reported:

> Snowdonia and Cumbria are all the year round resorts and at Christmas and Easter may be inconveniently crowded.

The crowding was indicative of better transport facilities making access to the mountains a good deal easier. North Wales was served by an express line that carried passengers direct from Manchester to Bethesda, a line Siegfried often came to use, and one which played its part in the important first meeting he had with C.F. Holland. A line north brought Cumbria closer to Manchester, for from Penrith one could travel by train to Whitehaven, a line that opened out both Keswick and Borrowdale. The mountaineering and climbing fraternity, however, kept themselves well away from the hordes of holiday makers. They were made up of a small group of 'Gentlemen Amateurs', who, more than likely, already knew each other socially outside the mountains. Arnold Lunn made the point in 1913:

'Mountaineers form, or should do, but for the cliques and envy, a very close freemasonry'.[2] The freemasonry insulated itself by taking over – quite literally – such places as the Wastwater Hotel or the Pen-y-Gwryd. Siegfried had no reason to exclude himself from the climbing *milieu* he found, even had he wished to do so, for it was the only way he was going to find partners worthy of his metal, and capable of following him up a climb when he really decided to extend himself.

Not only was the social composition of the climbing world different from today; so was the technical one, with none of the carefully designed workmanship which now goes into the manufacture of specialised equipment, nor were there safety devices available. The rope was more than likely to have been made of hemp, of doubtful strength, tied round the waist with a bowline, although anchoring by shoulder belay had increasingly replaced paying out the rope hand over hand round a conveniently located spike.

Siegfried was lucky to have come into rock-climbing at a stage in its evolution well suited to his genius; cometh the hour, cometh the man. Dividing climbing up into this phase or that is inevitably an arbitrary game, but a framework of some sort does help, and what is arguably still the best time-chart is the one proposed by H.M.Kelly and J.H.Doughty.[3] Their scheme divided rock-climbing into four main phases:

1. The Easy Way period.
   Up to 1880.
2. Gully and Chimney period.
   1880 to 1900.
3. Ridge and Arête period.
   1890 to 1905.
4. Slab and Wall period.
   1905 to the present day.

Kelly and Doughty readily conceded that a real problem exists when it comes to assigning any particular date to any particular phase or type of climbing. There are instances when a climb first ascended in one period ought, by virtue of its character and grade, to be assigned more appropriately to another. The instance they cited to illustrate the problem was that of Botterill's Slab, on Scafell. This Lake District classic, first led in boots by Botterill on June 3rd 1903, strictly comes under the Ridge and Arête period, but due to its sustained severity and exposed position, it is more characteristic of the Slab and Wall period. Botterill's Slab quickly gained a reputation for fierceness and danger, and it had to wait a full nine years until Siegfried came along to give it a second ascent. Still, granting the exceptions, the time-chart is a helpful one, allowing us to say that Siegfried came into rock-climbing during the Slab and Wall period, his second ascent of Botterill's being typical of the manner in which he would come to make Scafell Crag virtually an extension of himself.

For an undergraduate at the School of Engineering to get himself into a climbing club was not the simple process it is today (the Manchester University Mountaineering Club was formed in January 1928, when J.H. Doughty delivered the inaugural lecture on the subject of rock-climbing). Eventually, Siegfried was to join the Fell and Rock Climbing Club of the English Lake District, but the more obvious choice lay closer to hand, the Manchester-based Rucksack Club. Formed in 1902, with the object of facilitating 'walking tours, cave exploration and mountaineering in the British Isles and elsewhere, and bring into fellowship men who are interested in these pursuits', the Rucksack Club had strong ties with the University from the start. Siegfried's application for election to the Club was turned down by the Committee on the ground that he was under age. Strictly, according to the Rules, the decision was a correct one, but a golden opportunity had been lost, a point the Club came to recognise when it reduced the joining age from 21to19 as a result of the experience. Fortunately, in practice, it did not make a vast amount of difference, for Siegfried found himself in the thick of Club life, attending lectures and events at the Club's headquarters at the Albion Hotel.

It was by way of the Rucksack Club's Manchester network that Siegfried got to know J. Anton Stoop, a Swiss-German by background, who worked in a Manchester shipping office. The two men had much in common, for apart from being able to converse easily in German, both were brilliant rock technicians who mixed daring with prudence. Stoop became the leading tiger at Laddow Rocks, his first ascent of Leaf Crack and Cave Crack in boots being ahead of their time. Philip Brockbank made a special point of singling out the two men, which is interesting, because Brockbank had an intimate knowledge of the period and personally knew many of the chief climbers of the time.[4] Yet there appears to be no independent evidence of what the two men climbed together. Perhaps time ran out too early. Stoop was killed in October 1910, on the Eastern Arête of Nantlle y Garn, when boulders collapsed under him. The news of his death shook the Manchester climbing fraternity to its foundation. Stoop is buried in Llanllyfni churchyard, the first of Siegfried's friends to pay the ultimate price.

A much better documented Rucksack Club friendship is the one

Herford leading Laycock on Square Chimney, Wharncliffe

between Siegfried and Stanley Jeffcoat. Jeffcoat lived at Buxton, a tall, powerfully built and genial man, seven years older, although the age gap never seemed to bother either of them. The partnership between the two men was a staunch one, reaching its apotheosis on Scafell, where it is commemorated by the eponymous Jeffcoat's Ledge, a sign of the importance their friendship holds in the history of Lakeland climbing.

Jeffcoat's name is closely associated with a crag not very far from Buxton, Castle Naze, a gritstone headland magnificently situated 1,400 feet above sea level, the rampart of a hillfort defended by double banks and ditches. Jeffcoat was probably not the first to scramble on the crag, though he is often credited with having 'discovered' it, but he was certainly the man who introduced Siegfried to it. From Didsbury, Castle Naze was easy for Siegfried to reach either by bike or train, the rocks being only a mile-and-a-half south of Chapel-en-le-Frith station. The crag rapidly became one of his favourites. He would climb all through an afternoon and then drop down to the hamlet of Combs, where Mrs Elizabeth Martin, a kindly lady who mothered him, gave him tea. Mrs Martin, writing to Marie Herford said: 'I don't remember him ever camping here'. In the Spring Term of 1911, reacting from the pressure of exams, Siegfried cycled out and let off steam by soloing everything in sight. Castle Naze has its niche in British climbing history by being the crag on which Siegfried invented the Girdle Traverse. It was typical of his inventiveness, his feel for rock, his ability to see a line where others could not. This first of all Girdle Traverses is in miniature, 250 feet in length running roughly above middle height, its muted accretions splendid for an evening of late sun, but when Siegfried translated his lateral concept to the buttresses of Scafell it took on an altogether more daunting prospect.

Moving the Girdle Traverse from Castle Naze to the more formidable Scafell face only serves to underline the importance gritstone climbing holds in the evolution of rock-climbing. Peak District rock began to receive systematic attention towards the latter part of the nineteenth century. The founding-father of gritstone climbing was a Sheffield man, James William Puttrell, who as early as 1885 clambered on the Prow at Wharncliffe (often used as a training crag by Siegfried), and by the time the first edition of the *Climbers' Club Journal* came out in 1898, it was considered worthwhile to include an article by E.A. Baker entitled 'Practice Scrambles in Derbyshire'. Increasingly the abrasive millstone grit acted as a magnet for a growing number of Manchester enthusiasts Siegfried had started to meet. Gritstone climbing had not yet been accepted as a craft in its own right but was used for improving technique before transferring to the bigger crags elsewhere.

Herford leading Laycock on The Nose, Bramley's Traverse, Cratcliffe Tor

In this respect outcrop climbing played a vital role in pushing up standards. Kelly and Doughty emphasised the point:

> Gritstone climbs are short; but they have a high standard of severity and exposure; and the exiguous nature of their holds tends to produce a balance technique which is precisely what is required for face climbing of the delicate order. One need only cite the names of a few men who had their early training and experience on gritstone – Botterill, Herford, Kelly, Frankland, Pigott, Linnell, A.T.Hargreaves – to drive home the point.[5]

This meant that Manchester acted as an ideal base for any budding tiger with an eye on bigger things.

One of those lurking in the wings was John Laycock, 'the mysterious Laycock' as May called him, whom Siegfried first met early in his second term at the School of Engineering. Both men must have felt that destiny had played a not too subtle hand.

The story of how Siegfried and Laycock first met on Kinder Downfall is part of climbing folklore and a gift for the writers of guide books. It is a shame to spoil a good story, but a biographer has no choice but to deal in evidence, and in this instance the meeting is beset with contradictions surrounding it. The actual source for the story is Laycock himself, which on the face of it ought to be enough, but his detail is not always to be trusted, especially since he wrote two quite irreconcilable versions of what took place – or even when it did so. The lesser known of the two versions, but significantly the earliest one, is to be found hidden away in the *Manchester University Magazine* for 1916. Laycock wrote:

> The mountains to the mountaineer are not a sport but a religion – the religion. To me the mountains and Herford are indivisible. My last climb in the Lakes was with him a few days before I enlisted. In 1911, I was collecting facts about climbs on Kinder Scout and I had written to Sandiford as one supposed to know something about the place; he replied that all his climbing there had been done with Herford and arranged a meeting. When I arrived at the Downfall in the late afternoon of a warm February day – 11th February *1911* (my italics) – Herford was leading Sandiford up the *Great Chimney*, and Sandiford's appealing cries were wafted up the chimney to me at the top. Almost every smallest incident of that afternoon is fresher in my mind than the affairs of yesterday; Herford's long rather fair hair, his clear-cut fresh face above a soft grey jersey – almost every thing done and said. But even that day, the first, is little more living to me than any other day spent with him on the rocks.

Group at Castle Naze
Front left to right – Stanley Jeffcoat, John Laycock, A R Thompson.
Siegfried Herford
Back left to right – Unknown left, possibly Sandiford right

So far so good; however, while the smallest incident of that afternoon might have been fresher than the affairs of yesterday, by 1923 he had written a different account. In 1923, after Fergus Graham had asked Laycock to contribute a Preface to his *Recent Developments on Gritstone*, he wrote the version of the meeting that is normally adopted. This is what he said then:

> One fine afternoon in *1910* [again, my italics] I (tortuously) made my way up the North side of the Downfall ravine on Kinder Scout. Near *Professor's Chimney* I met a small climbing party, including a tall, strongly built young man with fair hair, blue eyes and regular features. Herford's manner was then, as always, pleasing and unassuming. That afternoon we climbed, among other things, the Varsity Crack. Herford had done little climbing, but he had always a deep and intense love of the hills and it was not difficult to predict that he would become a climber of the first order. Thenceforward we climbed together regularly.

That a meeting between Siegfried and Laycock on Kinder Downfall took place is not in dispute. The trouble arises due to Laycock's discrepancies.

It is hard to adjudicate between the two years Laycock gave for the Downfall meeting, 1910 or 1911, although the former fits more comfortably with everything else we know. The issue about the route Laycock said he found Siegfried climbing, on the other hand, demands closer scrutiny. There is a real difference in standard between the two of them, the Great Chimney graded at Hard Severe, while Professor's Chimney is of a lower order at Difficult, and if it was the harder of the routes Siegfried was on then the implication is striking, for to be capable of leading Hard Severe in winter at the age of nineteen was an outstanding level of climbing for 1910, one that would already have singled him out as a star performer. And he was certainly capable of it. Siegfried's jottings in his copy of *The Complete Mountaineer* show that in the same February of 1910, five days after his first meeting with Laycock on the Downfall, he went over to Wharncliffe Edge where he soloed the Cave Traverse, and then early in March, accompanied by C.E. Montague, he led Stonnis Crack at Black Rocks, one of those awkward gritstone Severes still regarded as something of a test piece. It is difficult to adjudicate between the two rock routes due to a lack of corroborative evidence, but we can do better with the discrepancies over the year, 1910 or 1911. The *Fell and Rock Climbing Club Journal* for 1911 recorded that both Siegfried and Laycock were present at the Club's July meet in 1910. The Journal also stated that Siegfried climbed on Dow Crag, leading a man named McConechy on the second ascent of O.G. Jones's Easter Gully (Severe). If he was capable of leading a climb of Severe standard in the July of 1910, it is reasonable to suppose he could have led Great Chimney in the February of that year.

In his earlier version of the Downfall meeting, Laycock said he had been collecting facts about climbs on Kinder Scout. This task ultimately led to the publication of his seminal guide, *Some Gritstone Climbs in Derbyshire and Elsewhere* (Refuge Printing Department, Manchester, 1913). His guide did a great deal to popularise gritstone climbing – and it resulted in a colossal row. Laycock had proposed to the Committee of the Rucksack Club that they cover the cost of publishing the guide, and having received a firm assurance from the Committee that they would do so, he went ahead collecting his facts as he said. By the end of 1911 his manuscript was ready for the printer. It was at this point that the Committee had a change of mind.

The change of mind was bound up with permits to climb issued by the landowners. Since the Enclosure Acts, wide areas of the open moors had been owned by a few wealthy people and used for the rearing of sheep and grouse shooting, particularly shooting. The owners jealously guarded their land from the invasion of climbers or walkers; much of the moorland was protected by gamekeepers, armed with sticks, which they were not afraid to use. Kinder Scout was forbidden territory, climbers operating surreptitiously, a constant cat-and-mouse game between them and the gamekeepers. But, in some cases, the owners did grant permits to climb and the Rucksack Club, with its well-oiled Establishment network, was well served by these private arrangements. That was the nub of the row. The authority on what happened is again Philip Brockbank:

> Pickstone in particular *(C.H.Pickstone, Club President 1914-1916, a solicitor by profession)* knowing that those crags were in preserved territory to which we *(i.e. the Rucksack Club)* were allowed occasional access, took fright at the thought that the publication of such a book over the Club's name might not only be considered as enticement to trespass but would almost certainly cause the irate landowners to refuse us any more permits. So the Committee withdrew its support. [6]

Laycock was devastated by the decision and a stormy altercation ensued. Pickstone, with his legal training, was technically almost certainly correct in saying the publication of the guide under the Club's imprimatur would be considered as an enticement to trespass, but Laycock insisted that the whole attitude of the Committee was morally wrong, a sell out to the big boys, and he promptly resigned from the Club. His guide book also became a further casualty of the affair. In 1911, when he was ready to go to print, he lacked the financial resources to press ahead himself, with the result that there was a two-year delay, until 1913.

When *Some Gritstone Climbs* finally emerged from the wars, Laycock dedicated it to Siegfried. Siegfried's own reaction to the fracas was to consolidate his friendship with Laycock. He might have pictured himself as one of Lietz's Guardians, and to that extent allied to the Establishment, but the liberal values of his upbringing led him to have little sympathy with the Enclosure Acts.

Stanley Jeffcoat, who was on the Rucksack Club Committee at the time, did not allow the *cause célèbre* to sour his affection for, or loyalty to the Club, and indeed in the following year, 1912, it was he who spearheaded the Club's historic initiative by opening the first climber's hut in the British Isles, an old shepherd's cottage in Cwm Eigiau under the shadow of Craig yr Ysfa. Nor did he let it interfere with his ever closer friendship with Siegfried. Since 1910, the friendship had had time to mature, and since that year the formidable trio of Siegfried, Jeffcoat and Laycock had started to leave its mark, and none of the three men was willing to allow the battle of the guide book to wreck an increasingly important partnership.

The best the trio achieved lay outside of the Peak District, but they had their say, for as Byne and Sutton rightly noted, 'the appearance of this powerful team in 1910 brought gritstone climbing to maturity'.[7] On Kinder they put up a series of routes which still remain some of the most popular: Varsity Crack, the Mermaid's Ridge, the Twin Chimneys, Downfall North Corner, and the Forked Chimneys. Almost certainly, the best of Siegfried's Kinder climbs is the eponymous Herford's Route on the Pagoda, between Edale Head rocks and Crowden Towers, a 'Very Severe' with an exit still capable of raising a sweat. The interest of the trio went well beyond the bounds of Kinder. The roaming extent of Siegfried's own activity is to be found in two publications. Stanley Jeffcoat's 'Climbs on Hen Cloud and the Roaches', in the *Rucksack Club Journal 1913*, is the first real guide to the two outcrops in which he noted cautiously that 'the exploration of these fine crags is now in progress and full details will have to be deferred to a later date'. The Roches in particular, with its great height and coarser rock, was a fine discovery then hardly touched. John Laycock had also been busy with the pen. In *The Field*, August 30th, 1913, he wrote what is effectively a summary of *Some Gritstone Climbs*, covering the six crags of Brassington, Castle Naze, Helsby, Hen Cloud, Laddow Rocks and Wharncliffe, accompanied by an illustration of each of the crags. The illustrations are of intense interest to us because they each show Siegfried leading up a climb. There was a route on the Downfall that Siegfried had gazed at with hungry eyes but which in the end he failed to subdue. *Some Gritstone Climbs* indicated the possibility:

> The most conspicuous feature is an extinguisher-shaped chimney of unyielding aspect about 60 feet high. So far as is known this remains a virgin and the whole face awaits an ardent investigator.

The unyielding line became known as Extinguisher Chimney, well in advance of its day, and forty years would pass before it finally conceded. The ardent investigators turned out to be the doughty Vin Dillon and Vin Desmond, nicknamed 'Dilly and Dally', although nobody knew which one was which. On August 28th, 1949, they had set out on one of their regular predatory sorties across the peat bogs of Kinder. They were at the top of their form, 'climbing anything with the faintest sign of a hold', with Vin Dillon just back from the Zmutt Ridge of the Matterhorn. Firstly, they examined Mill Hill, but found nothing to excite or detain them there; then, unmindful of the weight of history hanging in the balance, they found themselves at the foot of Extinguisher Chimney. Vin Dillon takes up the story:

> I got up into the lower section, which is easy enough, and jammed and wedged up, well inside. I remember being nicely wedged, about five/six feet in and about twenty feet up, looking outward to the wide slit that led to the upper section, and thinking 'ho hum'. We thought a belay would be handy and I was rather in favour of having Vin D. a bit closer. There was clearly the possibility of a thread on if we could wedge higher and thread a line through a narrow constriction right at the back of the lower cleft. We did (afterwards I claimed putting the thread in the back, high up, was the hardest part of the climb – don't think it's needed by today's climbers) and outwards I wedged until the next move was fresh air and there was no option but to break onto the upper section and go for it. So it was sort of lean out, reach up, find holds, swing out and pedal up. A hand jamb, good holds and toe jamb in quick succession and Extinguisher Chimney had been swept.

It was desperate stuff in the best gritstone tradition, 'extremely awkward and strenuous', recorded Vin Desmond in his meticulously kept diary. Desmond's own first attempt to follow proved abortive, leaving him with a badly torn shirt, but he succeeded with his second go by facing right.[8]

As well as exploring gritstone, Siegfried tried his hand on the much feared carboniferous limestone. He was one of the few who attempted the ascent of High Tor Gully, but hardly with the approval of Laycock, who had warned the reader of *Some Gritstone Climbs* that 'mountain limestone is beyond the border line of safety'. This did not stop Siegfried having a go at the famous Ilam Rock, in Dovedale. This was one of Siegfried's later climbs, in August, 1914, and the account we have of it was written by A.R. Thomson, a resolute second on any climb, who shared with Edward VII a passion for motoring.[9]

There was a general feeling that Ilam Rock had not had a proper ascent. During the August Bank Holiday of 1903, the egocentric Samuel Turner had been up it, lured as much by the show as he had been by the danger. The purists insisted that Turner had cheated. Instead of climbing the pinnacle clean, he threw a rope over the top, and encouraged by the cheers of the watching crowd, he pulled himself up hand over hand, then, once on top, he had the audacity to stand on his head. Turner was a showman to his fingertips, but despite all his artificial manipulations, it was something of an achievement even to have tackled this limestone monolith which had such a fearsome reputation for danger. Just how fearsomely justified that reputation was had been confirmed by various parties since Turner who had endeavoured to climb Ilam Rock 'clean'; all had been defeated. That is how matters stood when Siegfried appeared on the scene.

Siegfried arrived at Dovedale in some style as a passenger in A.R. Thomson's Lagonda, accompanied with a mutual friend named Peacock. 'Ilam Rock', wrote Thomson, 'stands on steeply-sloping ground and is most easily to be attacked from the back by its north side'. This is what Siegfried did. An overcast sky deteriorated into spitting rain which quickly made the rock uncomfortably greasy. A vertical pitch took Siegfried to a prominent sapling roughly 30 feet from the ground. He stood on the trunk of the tree, belayed, and brought Peacock up to a recess some six feet below. At the recess, limestone lived up to its reputation when Peacock's foothold broke off and left him hanging by his hands to tufts of grass above his head. The belay held. Siegfried again found himself leading on vertical rock until he reached a tricky recess where he waited for twenty minutes on the same small foothold before attempting the next move, his usual mixture of daring and prudence prevailing.

Cautiously, testing each hold as he went, he gained a slightly sloping upward ridge, so narrow that he sat astride it, and once on top he brought up Peacock and Thomson. They searched the airy ridge for the penny Turner said he had left on it, but without success. The three of them got back to the ground by a complicated manoeuvre which enabled them to retrieve the rope behind them. Ilam Rock had been led cleanly for the first time, but it had been an odd climb, and certainly a dangerous one, and it leaves the question as to whether or not it had been justified. Walt Unsworth has expressed the view that the hair-raising nature of Siegfried's ascent was sufficient to deter most climbers and he reckoned that the event retarded 'the development of limestone climbing for almost four decades'.[10] That said, it has also to be seen as one further illustration of Siegfried's willingness to strike out and anticipate the future, his quest for modernity, for there was no other climber around at the time capable of tackling such a lead on limestone.

Siegfried was highly concentrated in whatever he did, prepared for whatever sacrifice his activity demanded, and he climbed with electrifying intensity. In 1912, his final year as an undergraduate at the School of Engineering, he packed in a hundred days of actual climbing. It is reasonable to assume from this that he put his academic work second, and that it was bound to suffer; but that was far from the case. His examination results speak for themselves: in each of the three academic years he came out top in mathematics; in two of them he was also top in physics, metallurgy, and geology; again in his second year, the only year in which he took German language, he also emerged top – although hardly unexpectedly. The fact of the matter is that Siegfried was never lower than second place in any subject throughout his course. After finishing top of his year, he left the School of Engineering with a postgraduate scholarship, which he used for aeronautical research at the Royal Aircraft Factory, Farnborough. He never lost his contact with Manchester, or with the Manchester climbing scene, but he returned to be close to the Surrey Downs he had got to know as a boy at Boxgrove House School.

CHAPTER SEVEN

THE HOME CRAGS OF ERYRI

Siegfried's lasting affection for his birthplace, together with the long family walks he undertook as a child around the local hills, implanted in him a feeling that part of him was rooted in Wales and he loved every nuance of its mountains and the land. When he wandered the wild swathes of the Carneddau, and gazed across the haze of water fading west beyond Anglesey, it is possible to imagine him remembering the sea and horizon he saw as a boy from the top of Constitution Hill. Trevor Jones and Geoff Milburn noted in their history of Welsh rock-climbing that Siegfried's 'fame was not to be earned in Wales'.[1] They were right of course; but fame was not what he went to Wales for; he entered Wales as if he was returning home and he went there for sustenance.

By the time Siegfried had begun to explore the Welsh crags more seriously, a degree of anxiety had started to build up at home, with his parents worrying about what he was doing. From the day Siegfried scaled Napes Needle in the summer of 1908, his parents appreciated that their son would rock-climb at a reasonable level, but, following his meeting with Laycock and Jeffcoat, things had taken a more serious turn. They might not be aware of all the finer points, but they were sufficiently knowledgeable about mountains and climbing to grasp the main thrust of what was happening, and they sensed danger. Not for the first time, it was left to May to pour oil on troubled water. On one occasion, while she was enjoying a brief holiday at Devil's Bridge, she wrote to her father who was working in France. In her letter she expressed the hope that her mother did not feel anxious about what Siegfried intended to do in Wales: 'He is not', she said, 'going to climb in the strict sense of the word'. But that was precisely what he did intend to do, as she knew full well, and there was no point in trying to cover up the fact.

The sort of escapade his parents had in mind was what happened when he returned to Cader Idris, the mountain he had been up with his father when he was still a mere toddler of four. Back at Didsbury, he and Laycock had mulled over a scheme to walk from Manchester to Windermere in under 24 hours. The walk itself never happened, but as training for it Siegfried tramped into Wales, covering a distance of 63 miles in 16 hours, only calling a halt out of sheer boredom. He slept the night in the open, tucked under a haystack, to be rudely awakened next morning by an irate Welsh farmer who sent him scurrying off. Once he arrived at Cader Idris, entirely alone in true Rose Pope style, he climbed the Great Gully of Craig y Cau, on the right of the steep Pencoed Pillar. The technical standard, graded Hard Very Difficult today, was well within his capabilities, but it is a long climb, wet and loose, one of those threatening places where a chunk of frost-splintered rock can hive off at any moment. From the lichenous inner recess of the gully he could see right down to the gloomy waters of the lake 1000 feet below. There was no margin for error, he was on his own, without the possibility of a rescue should an injury occur, such as loose rock collapsing on him or under him. He allowed himself no such forebodings, the Prince, as it were, was on his Chair, but it was the sort of thing that did little to calm parental nerves.

The first indication we have of Siegfried rock-climbing in North Wales is found in the notes he made in his copy of *The Complete Mountaineer*. He recorded a ten-day visit to the Ogwen Valley, between April 7th -16th, 1910, adding that he was on his own throughout the entire period. Ogwen was a natural choice. That same year, J.M. Archer Thomson had published his pioneering guide, *Climbing in the Ogwen District*, confirming how, alongside Lliwedd, the area had grown into a focal point for Welsh climbing. Ogwen in those days, whether in sun or with twilight rain running up the valley, was a place where a tent would stand among the old simplicities, a rough edge and a touch of wildness which has since gone, with much of the rock untamed and untouched by the climber's boot. The area offered the perfect foil for Siegfried's penchant for solitary climbing and he clearly took full advantage of it. He started out on April 7th by scaling the clean rock of the Milestone Buttress, moved round to the East Face of Tryfan where he climbed what he called Central Buttress, now better known as 1st Pinnacle Rib, and ended by trying his luck on the lower half of the Monolith Crack. The next day, the 8th, we find him opening the day on the Ordinary Route of Idwal Slabs, then prudently withdrawing at the top pitch of the Devil's Kitchen, before wandering round to Tryfan again where he ascended South Buttress. These scrambles, as he called them, were typical of the way he went about a mountain area, shifting from this place to that, probing and testing, saturating himself in the nuances of the rock world in which he found himself. He was not so specific about the remainder of the visit, contenting himself with a generalised note: 'Odd scrambles in the district – alone'.

In the May of 1911, Siegfried and Laycock stationed themselves in the

Ogwen Valley, where they were joined by R. Hodgkinson, W.R. Milligan and a young Manchester friend named Morley Wood, who was later to feature in the history of Clogwyn Du'r Arddu's East Buttress. Archer Thomson's guide had singled out the cliffs of Glyder Fach, recommending the crag because he considered the rock to be steeper, less broken by terraces, and offered climbs of greater difficulty. On the strength of Archer Thompson's judgement, Siegfried and Laycock set off for Glyder Fach, first climbing the Direct Route, which they followed by tackling Oblique Gully. For whatever reason, they were not in an exploratory mood, and decided to concentrate their attention lower down the valley.

Siegfried, Laycock, Hodgkinson, Milligan, and Morley Wood assembled the next day at the foot of the Gribin Facet, a real turn of the century crag, where there was much squeezing and fun and laughter in the famous 'thrutch' of the Monolith Crack, dismissed by Siegfried as enjoyable gymnastics, and then he started to look around for virgin rock. It was at this point that the Herford Crack was climbed, not so much a vague crack as a vague location, its precise whereabouts baffling even Colin Kirkus. If, as Kirkus supposed, it is the vertical 30-feet crack just to the right of the start of Flake Crack, then it bears the hallmark of a Siegfried route. There is no vagueness about the thoroughly attractive Slab Climb, the longest line on the crag, running up the obvious East Wing. There is a photograph of Siegfried leading the first ascent of Slab Climb. The real prize of the day, by far the best discovery on the Facet, was Zig-Zag, led by Siegfried, seconded by Laycock, and followed by Hodgkinson and Milligan. It is a bit of a mystery why Morley Wood was not also on the climb. Laycock described Zig-Zag in detail:

> Immediately to the right of the Monolith Crack is now the Zig-Zag Climb, marked by a cairn. A corner is ascended for 30 feet to the level of a small shelf, which slopes upwards to the right. The crack above the shelf is denuded of its once lovely ferns, but its first few feet are still decidedly difficult, and altogether 80 feet of rope is required to reach a sentry-box. A heathery glacis now calls for care; at its topmost corner, arrived at by bearing to the left, are two cracks of which we selected that on the left-hand side. A single pillar intervenes between this and the top pitch of the Monolith. A strong position is obtained at the foot of the crack by reclining on the patch of grass and inserting unoccupied members in receptive fissures. This ultimate pitch is also decidedly difficult.

Ron James has reminded us that the climb still commands respect:

Herford leading Laycock on the first ascent of Slab Climb, Gribin Facet, Ogwen, in May 1911

The best route on the cliff, steep and open and on good rock. It is hard and care is needed to protect the V-chimney, adequately. [2]

Zig-Zag is evidence of a growing maturity about Siegfried's climbing, a sharp eye for a line, and a willingness to round off cleanly.

The visit to Ogwen had been a short one but it was not to be long before Siegfried was back in Wales.

During the first half of August, again in 1911, he and Laycock pitched a tent by the side of Llyn Teyrn, off the Miner's track. What we know of this trip is best contained in a letter by Siegfried, dated September 4th, written when he got back to Didsbury, and sent to the Professor who was again away working in Norway. From the sound of it, right from the start, everything seems to have gone wrong. Siegfried explained to his father:

> We first had a week in Wales, as perhaps you know, camping near Llyn Llydaw, and in full view of Lliwedd. We pitched our tent on the Sunday in the pouring rain and in pitch darkness, aided only by a bicycle lamp, and it was a very weird business altogether. I had stupidly left my tent poles behind and we had to put up with two broomsticks about the required size so that we had to positively crouch inside the tent. The week went off quite well, only the weather was rather unsettled and prevented our doing any of the greater Lliwedd climbs which require perfect conditions.

They did, in fact, succeed in getting up a dripping Slanting Buttress, but the original intention behind the camp had been far reaching, a measure of how far Siegfried's ambition had enlarged. The plan had been to spend the week by completing every climb on the cliff, 30 of them all told in those days, equivalent to methodically ticking off everything on Clogwyn Du'r Arddu today. The weather had other ideas and they were not able to put their plan into action. They used a lull in the rain to good effect, exploring the Cwm Dyli defile, which is when they stumbled across an open and attractive slab, christening their new climb on it the Teyrn Ridge. Finding themselves increasingly messy, damp, and uncomfortable in the low tent, they packed off to Ogwen again where they hoped life might prove somewhat easier. Here they climbed the Devil's Kitchen, left alone by other climbers because of its reputation for gloom and danger and friable rock. Siegfried told his father he considered the sinister reputation to be exaggerated:

> We did do several good things, however, among which was the complete ascent of the Devil's Kitchen, which was not nearly so dangerous as it is made to be by people who have not done it.

Becoming more and more his own man, he was content to make up his own mind about a climb, and not be put off by hearsay. Once the weather brightened up, Siegfried and Laycock went back to Glyder Fach, a cliff much to their fancy. They inspected the pear-shaped slab at the lower termination of Main Gully, and, much to their surprise, found the rock unexpectedly dry, so they got ready for action. Laycock wore scarpetti, but Siegfried's shoes were in ribbons, so he had to content himself with stockings. Siegfried led two new climbs, Alpha and Beta, on what is now Alphabet Slab. These two delicate routes marked the end of climbing in Wales that year.

In the July of the following year, 1912, Siegfried and Laycock, now inseparable, were again in the Ogwen Valley. This visit was more memorable for a first meeting, rather than for any climbing, because it was on this occasion that Siegfried came across C.F. Holland. For a description of how the meeting happened, we have to project forward, to June 1st, 1918, to when Holland was staying at the Pen-y-Gwryd. He was then a 2nd Lieutenant, recuperating, wreathed in a plaster-cast from shoulder to elbow, the bone of his right arm having been splintered by a German bullet. Despite his incapacity, he was able to write, and in a letter to Marie Herford thanking her for photographs of Siegfried she had sent him, he explained how the two met:

> We first met on a train from Bangor to Bethesda when we sat in opposite corners in the same carriage and subsequently sharing a trap to Ogwen. I shall never forget his kindness in making me a member of his already large party.

Holland was an Olympian, described by Dorothy Pilley as 'short, tough, virile, and, as far as I could see, not knowing what fear meant'.[3] There was certainly no fear in his climbing; H.M. Kelly explained how he climbed with an *elan* that positively unnerved the timid. He had an unquenchable zest for new routes, always the right man to have around when the going got tight, the depth of his staunchness becoming legendary during his seven-hour vigil at the Oval during the siege of Central Buttress. Decidedly a character, this man who had won a Military Cross and Bar in the First World War, volunteered in the Second as an unpaid Lance-Corporal instructing Commandos in the finer points of mountain warfare. This service came to an abrupt end when, his stock with authority already at a low ebb, he was found scaling the outside of Winchester Cathedral. Holland was one of the most enduring of the Edwardians, with more than a touch of mountain mysticism in his outlook, and he continued to climb into ripe old age.

Little has been recorded about what Siegfried's large party did. Certainly, Siegfried himself, Laycock and Holland went back up to Glyder Fach. They made the first ascent of Square Chimney, on the extreme left-hand edge of the cliff, but it was such a hopelessly scrappy route that when Kirkus and Graham Macphee went to repeat it in 1932, they gave it a miss, and turned to Alpha instead.

Siegfried paid one further visit to Wales in 1912. This time it was a family affair, when he joined with his mother and sister, the Professor being away on his travels farther afield.

The Herfords based themselves on Trefriw, with its pump house and paddle steamers plying between the local quay and Colwyn Bay, a fashionable middle-class spa built on the supposed quality of the water and the never-ending search for cures. The town was Edwardian boudoir territory, all fragility and delicacy of manners, where the pianoforte took precedence over the climbing rope. Siegfried acquiesced, no doubt because Trefriw had been selected to suit his mother, and he very much wanted her to enjoy the most of her holiday. Siegfried and May had bicycles with them, and on one day they set off on a long, circular ride, taking them to Llanberis and Caernarvon Castle.

In one note on the holiday, Siegfried recorded that the ladies had taken off for Conway together, and although he did not explain what he got up to in the meanwhile, needs must when the devil drives and there was always the climber lurking underneath. This reserved one day for brother and sister to climb Tryfan together, May saying how thoroughly relaxed she felt on 'the mild but exhilarating rocks', thanks to 'S's very careful help and leadership'. There was always a caring and thoughtful side to Siegfried's character, although ever since they shared the magic of planet Mars together, she had had a brilliant ability to bring it out, and see that side of him.

Before the holiday ended, Siegfried had a day's climbing on his own, when he trudged over to Craig yr Ysfa to tackle the Great Gully. The walk took him three hours so it was one o'clock before he got to grips with the climb. In a letter to his father he went into considerable detail and said how much the gully had impressed him:

> The gully consists of 10 pitches or steep rocky portions separated by easy grassy stretches. The highest of these pitches is some 55 ft. Two or three of these I found decidedly trying, but I was used to that kind of work from Wharncliffe and other places, so I managed to conquer them. The worst place in the whole course was only 12 ft high. In the upper part of the gully the walls were very high and

perpendicular, and the view like Deep Ghyll on Scafell, only a good deal narrower. At the top some boulders jammed between walls formed a large cave, and this was the most interesting though by no means the hardest part of the course. I reached the top at 3.30 and wended my way home in a very bedraggled condition.

The Great Gully of Craig yr Ysfa, described by Archer Thomson as 'exceedingly difficult and delectable', is a harder technical climb than the Great Gully of Craig y Cau, but safer and less exposed to risk. It is interesting that Siegfried thought that his previous training on gritstone had prepared him to master the harder pitches. What were his thoughts as he emerged bedraggled from the dark recess of the gully, a lone and isolated figure looking down into the wild Cwm Eigiau below? He would have been able to see the little shepherd's cottage which his close friend, Stanley Jeffcoat, had just finished converting into a Rucksack Club hut, the first climbers' hut in the British Isles, and an example typifying the way both men contributed to the history of homeland climbing.

CHAPTER EIGHT

HERCULES ON SKYE

Again, in the summer of 1912, after finding himself confined in the peacock environs of Trefriw, but still flush from his effort in the Great Gully of Craig yr Ysfa, Siegfried linked up with Laycock, and the two of them left Didsbury to travel north to Skye.

It was a wonderful moment of anticipation for both of them. Ever since Charles Pilkington's daring first ascent of the Inaccessible Pinnacle in 1880, and the white-haired Norman Collie discovered the Cioch in 1899, when the huge rock cast its shadow at sundown over the vast precipice of Sron na Ciche, the rugged Cuillin had become the rock-climber's Mecca. Samuel Johnson may have dismissed the Cuillin as 'laborious' and 'dangerous', but the rough gabbro rock was a dream, talked about in lyrical terms.

Today an outrageous bridge and well-made road have made Skye easy to reach. It was anything but easy in Siegfried's day. Back at Didsbury, when plans were being made, it almost seemed as if Skye retained the wild remoteness of the heroic age of the Norsemen. The attempt to get there could take on the atmosphere of an expedition. Public transport, train or ferry, were unreliable and erratic, connections could so easily be lost, and a carefully worked-out programme jeopardised in the process. Just how true that was, Siegfried and Laycock were to find out for themselves.

Hitherto, all we have known about the Skye episode has come from the pen of Laycock, in an account he wrote for the 1914 edition of the *Fell and Rock Climbing Club Journal*. His opening gambit could hardly have been more cryptic:

> The mists rolled down again and anon we landed, after a suitable Odyssey of adventure – perhaps the labours of Hercules would be a comparison more apt.

He left it at that. What Odyssey befell them? How did the labours of Hercules come into it? Laycock leaves us none the wiser. We are left to surmise that something must have happened, although Laycock offered us no help, and all we can do is ponder what he might have referred to.

Fortunately, however, late one night aboard a fishing smack, heaving uncomfortably off the Isle of Rum, Siegfried wrote an amazing letter to his father, recounting in vivid detail the whole story of their adventure and labours of Hercules. The letter is headed 'Fishing Smack. Isle of Rhum.

Tuesday Night', with no date attached, but as they had left Manchester on Friday, August 15th, he must have written it on the 19th:

> We left Manchester 11 o'clock on Friday night, and changed at Wigan, and got a train north at 12.30. We had to change at Carlisle at 3 a.m. and get a train which had connection with a North British Railway train at Crianlarich, between Killin and Oban. Owing however to the lateness of the train, we missed it by a minute, and had the pleasure of seeing our other train sail out before our own eyes. This excluded all chance of getting to Skye till Monday, as there were no more boats. We therefore continued our journey as far as the Bridge of Orchy, where we sent on our main baggage to Mallaig, and tramped the 13 miles to Kingshouse at the head of Glencoe, at the foot of Buachaille Etive. We got to Kingshouse about 5 p.m. and after tea strolled over to the rocks, but did not do much as it was raining. The next day was better, and we did the very fine Crowberry Ridge, a magnificent climb. Got back to Kingshouse at 3 p.m. and then walked back to Bridge of Orchy, where we spent the night in a sort of outhouse belonging to the station – not comfortable, and not much sleep.

None of that astonishing narrative is mentioned by Laycock. He did say they were 'fresh from the Crowberry Ridge', but with no hint as to why, or how it came about they found themselves on the Buachaille instead of heading direct to Skye.

Siegfried and Laycock clearly enjoyed their excursion to the Buachaille, for while the delay in getting to Skye was obviously a source of frustration, carrying out a comparatively early ascent of Crowberry Ridge provided ample compensation. At the time, large areas of the Scottish Highlands remained virtually undiscovered from a climbing point of view, retaining the lure of the unknown. From 1899, when the Scottish Mountaineering Club was formed, a group of illustrious pioneers made summer and winter climbs of high calibre, but there was still an element of exploration even in their activity. The head of Glencoe, guarded by the Buachaille itself, retained a brooding remoteness, and Siegfried and Laycock were isolated as they weaved their way up the grey rib of rock.

The dark gully to the right of Crowberry Ridge had been mastered three years previously by a party led by the redoubtable Harold Raeburn, while the steep and exposed Rannoch Wall would have to wait three more decades before a route could be found up it. After a long day of walking and climbing, the two of them spent an uncomfortable night in a station outhouse, something more reminiscent of a latter generation of climbers, the colourful and impecunious Glaswegian lads of the 1930s, vividly brought to life in Alastair Borthwick's *Always a Little Further*, only, in this instance, their place was taken by two middle-class men, one of them a professed Guardian in the Hermann Lietz mould.

The uncomfortable night at Bridge of Orchy by no means ended their misadventures. Siegfried again takes up the story:

> We intended the next morning to catch the train which we had missed on Saturday, and for that purpose had to go by train to the previous station as the other train did not stop at the Bridge of Orchy. We managed that alright, not without a row with the station master as to tickets. When we got to Fort William we were told we would wait 6 minutes there. We therefore dashed off to the refreshment room, and emerged 4 minutes later to find our train had already departed. Skye put off another day and Ben Nevis impossible as all our things were in the compartment. We therefore booked on the next train to Mallaig, getting there at 2 p.m. Here we saw the Coolin hills, and after talking to sailors, decided to get put across to Armadale, 6 miles across, where we could get a cart to take us to the Point of Sleat, whence fishermen would get us to our destination, Glen Brittle, that evening. This seemed tempting, so we took it on, and had a lovely sail across. We had some trouble in getting a cart, which eventually took us most of the way to the Pt. of Sleat. The road was bad for the last three miles and the man needed a great deal of persuasion to take us on. We eventually stopped one mile short, where we camped. We also found out that the fishermen, Martin by name, were away, although the man had assured us they were at home. It was 6 in the evening. Early next morning therefore Laycock walked back to Armadale and wired the man at Mallaig who had brought us over to meet us at Pt. of Sleat with boat which he had promised to do if wired to. I, in the meanwhile, packed up belongings and proceeded to carry them down to the Pt. of Sleat – an arduous business. Laycock returned, having had a row with the owner of the cart which on the journey back had both its shafts broken and wished us to pay etc. etc. which J.L. stoutly refused to do. Well, we waited and waited at the Pt. of Sleat, but no boat came, and we at last gave up all hope of it. There we were, nicely landed, no boat, no cart, no food, and a ton of baggage. And it was raining. We then accepted the hospitality of the kindly fishermen's wife who gave us to eat and drink. Then, about 2 in the afternoon, the fishermen turned up, having had the

wire given them by the man we had wired to, who could not come. The best they could do for us was to take us to Rhum, where we could catch a steamer next morning, a weekly one to Soay, a small island off Skye near Glen Brittle, and thence get ferried across. This we agreed upon readily and had a pretty rough crossing in the smack. 3 hours, very enjoyable. On getting to Rhum, we found the steamer did not call regularly at all owing to a row with the owner of the island (Rhum). We therefore wired to it at another port to call here, which we assumed it had to do in that case; but any time between 11 p.m. and 6 a.m., a nice night in prospect. However, we pitched our tent at 7 p.m. and had a good meal, when the Martins came along and said we had better get aboard their smack again so as to be quite ready for the steamer when it came.This we forthwith did, being rowed back in the black of night, so here we are in a small cabin holding 6 men – 4 of them snoring, J.L. and I writing. We hope with luck to get to our destination tomorrow, but one never knows. However, we have had our moneys worth so far, even if not much climbing.

Of the twelve classic 'Labours of Hercules', perhaps the tenth is the closest to this drawn-out saga, the one in which Hercules had to get himself to Erythia, a western island, so as to bring back the cattle of Geryon.

Delay in news from Skye again caused alarm bells to ring at Didsbury. This time roles were reversed, the Professor working at home, Marie Herford away, visiting family at Bremen. When, eventually, Siegfried's fishing smack letter arrived, followed shortly afterwards with a postcard, he forwarded them to Bremen as quickly as he could:

At last the Prodigal has let us hear from him, and his prodigalism does not seem to be very grave after all. One did not – and really could not – allow for their remoteness. The letter and card both came this morning, but one seems to have been written on Wednesday week and the other on Sunday! I am sending them with this scrap by the early post; I thought of telegraphing, but that would only have alarmed you, and there was no real ground for anxiety as any accident must have become known. Still, I was beginning to wonder whether, in this weather, among the distant crags of Skye, two tourists who were not living in an hotel might not disappear without anyone noticing.

How far Siegfried would have been happy to be passed off as a tourist, we must let pass, but the level of parental anxiety is all too evident.

The two of them must have been mightily relieved when the mists rolled down and 'anon we landed'. It had been a long haul. They were not indeed, as the Professor said, living in an hotel, if only for the simple reason that in Glen Brittle there was no hotel to be had, only, at the sea end of the glen, Glen Brittle Lodge, a one-time shooting lodge of the MacLeods. Where, on the other hand, they actually pitched their tent is hard to fathom. Laycock wrote that they camped 'about 3 or 4 miles south west of Glen Brittle, in the middle of a bog'. A bog could have been anywhere, for the flattened uplands above the flanks which sink down to the sea are one vast bog, but 3 or 4 miles south west of the glen would seem to place them somewhere around the Loch Eynort region. This tends to be confirmed by the amount of walking they did before reaching the climbs, although why they put themselves so far away from the main ridge it is hard to say.

The Professor's letter made a reference to how bad the weather had been at Didsbury. It was no better in Skye. The start of real climbing coincided with the onset of rain, pouring down in torrents, and it carried on doing so with that peaty smell it seems to reserve for Skye. High on Sron na Ciche, in the vicinity of the Cioch, the rain caught them out. Laycock again:

> The great slab was covered with surface water to the depth of nearly half an inch, and the Eastern Gully became a river with pools, in which – I do not exaggerate – we could almost have stood submerged.

He did not exaggerate. Eastern Gully in full spate, when wavelets blow over the furls of rock, takes on the appearance of a white-water rapid. He seems to have taken an inverted pride in recalling their constant drenchings. He wrote in the 1916 *Manchester University Magazine*:

> Each day we trudged miles, climbed something – anything. Many days we carried huge loads and every day got wet with no ordinary wetness ... The worst part of that holiday was putting on wet breeches each morning. One night a howling gale (and rain) carried off our flysheet. We had to get up, strip stark naked (to keep our pyjamas a little dry – they were our only clothes not wet) and go out into the night to secure that fly-sheet. That wind was more than a little thin.

Wet or not, they climbed Slanting Gully on Sgurr a' Mhadaidh, and scaled the Inaccessible Pinnacle by the two hardest routes.

Included in the *Manchester University Magazine* is an account of a fascinating little incident he omitted from the *Fell and Rock Climbing Club Journal*. Laycock remembered how, on a day that for once turned out to be fine, they were on the Third Pinnacle of Sgurr nan Gillean:

Siegfried Herford on the Third Pinnacle of Sgurr nan Gillean in 1912.
Note the laid, hemp rope and the clinker-nailed boots.

In Skye occurred the only time Herford was ever really annoyed with me. On a fine day we climbed the Third Pinnacle of Sgurr nan Gillean, from Bhasteir Cove. Herford walked up the difficult slab with ease but spent some time on the cave pitch. (This pitch was once thought impossible without a shoulder from below and an additional push from the third man.) He came down for a rest and said he might want a shoulder. While he rested I went up to look at the place, and finding that it suited my style I went on and did it. He was annoyed for almost two hours, which time I spent grovelling apologetically before him. At no other time have I ever seen him really in a bad temper, not though we have often been alone together for a week.

Bad temper is one way of putting it, although others might recognise the 'special needs' syndrome, and while he had got beyond what May had called outbursts of impetuous violence, it is easy to believe that for two hours he disappeared into one of his long and unnerving silences. Laycock had been guilty of nothing. It was a perfectly natural thing for Laycock to find he could lead the cave pitch, and then go ahead and do it, but that is not how Siegfried saw it. He used climbing as a vehicle to bring his mind and body into focus, the manoeuvre he had found so hard to do as a boy, and he was not going to have Laycock, or anybody else, usurp his private space. Both of them were strong characters, but of the two Siegfried was much the stronger, and all Laycock could do was to give ground apologetically.

The rogue rain did nothing to quench their enthusiasm, and towards the end of their stay on Skye they found themselves at the opposite end of the ridge to Sgurr nan Gillean, probing the hidden Coire nan Laogh, the Corrie of the Calves, sandwiched between Gars-bheinn and Sgurr nan Eag. Here they spotted three unclimbed gullies, now known as the West, Central, and East respectively, but which they called A., B., and C. The West and East turned out to be easy, almost nonevents, but Central Gully put up more resistance. This time Siegfried did the leading. He started left of a square chockstone lodged in the gully, ascended an awkwardly greasy slab, traversed left above it, and finished off by taking the long chimney at the top. It was a climb in a minor key, but fittingly, it allowed the two friends to leave their mark on another mountain area.

CHAPTER NINE

A FELL AND ROCK MAN

The Fell and Rock Climbing Club had a romantic start on the shores of Goat's Water. In 1906, a group of friends sat chatting by the lake, having come down from climbing on Dow Crag, when it struck them that the time had come for a club 'with the sole object of fostering a love of mountaineering and the pastime of rock-climbing in the English Lake District'. They planted their sapling well. Developments which have taken place in the Lake District since then without the Fell and Rock knowing about it, or being in some way involved, are hardly worth talking about.

The Fell and Rock elected Siegfried into membership on February 24th, 1912, his proposer almost inevitably being John Laycock and his seconder A.R. Thomson. Competence was expected of an applicant, but in those days no formal qualification was required for membership, and thus the Club has no record of what Siegfried wrote in support of his application.

Election sealed an association with the Club going back to 1910. On the surface, nobody appeared less of a club man than Siegfried, with none of the qualities for mixing easily in the social life a club demands. 'To all but his intimates', Laycock said of him, 'he was rather reserved'. Reserved is an understatement; others thought him austere and remote. Yet this distant and silent man was able to draw to himself a tight circle of long-standing friends, a group of brilliant climbers, men of style and cultured mind, testingly select, and in some cases the best of their day. The paradox is that he took his membership of the Fell and Rock with the utmost seriousness and thoroughly enjoyed the social bonding.

One of the friendships, an absolutely crucial one, was with George Sansom. The two first met in 1911. The distinguished Lake District writer, A. Harry Griffin, described George Sansom as a 'shortish, slightly sunburned man who smoked what looked like a home-made cherry wood pipe'. [1] The chances are high that the pipe was home-made, for Sansom was a renaissance man with a prodigy of gifts, a brilliant wood and metal worker as well as being a pioneer of photo-micrography. At the time he and Siegfried met he was Derby Scholar in Zoology. Sansom came into climbing after being inspired by A.E.W. Mason's evocative novel *Running Water*, and when, in 1907, at the age of 19, he paid his first visit to Wasdale his fate was sealed. It was the beginning of a lifelong love affair, an integral part of his life to which he returned to every season, always climbing

Hopkinson's Gully, his favourite route, on the first day of a holiday. Siegfried's respect for his gentlemanly friend never wavered. Sansom, in his turn, is on record as saying that no quarrel or disagreement ever marred their potent partnership, and he wrote of Siegfried:

> He was tall, slim and graceful in movement, and when I read Kipling's description of Kamal's son, 'That dropped from a mountain crest – he trod the ling like a buck in Spring and looked like a lance at rest', I felt it was a suitable description of S.W. Herford ... Herford was a most generous climber. He was much better than I was, yet he often suggested that I should lead. He also gave me the credit for new climbs which I had only planned and he had led. I remember when we did the Girdle Traverse of Scafell, H.E. Gibson was writing up the account of it in the Wasdale book and he rightly put Herford's name first. Herford protested and said, "Sansom planned the whole thing, he ought to come first". I supported Gibson. At that time I would not have tried to lead Botterill's Slab. I was perhaps better at planning new routes but Herford was the bolder climber. He was essentially a very safe leader and I never felt any anxiety when he was climbing. [2]

Sansom was being characteristically chivalrous, for the two men complemented each other, and when Sansom's turn came to lead he did so in his own right. Their partnership was indisputably one of the greatest British rock-climbing has seen. Unlike his friend, Sansom lived a long life, with an exceedingly happy marriage to Dorothy Vivien Dodgson, and dying in 1980 in the house near Godalming he had lived in for sixty years.

In the April of 1912, after receiving the welcome news that he was now a Fell and Rock man, he wrote to May in Oxford. He told her how he had been 'cinematographed' by the Abraham brothers climbing the Napes Needle. He found being a film star as gruelling as it was frustrating:

> By this time the sun had come round onto the right side of the Needle, and S. (Sansom) and I were ready once more to be cinema'd. I led up this. As I went up the first Crack, which is a fag under any conditions, Abraham realised that his film would be wound off before I got to the top of it; 'Faster, faster', shouted A. from the dress circle, and I made most Herculean efforts, and was terrible afraid of getting jammed or dropping off, both of which are possible when one has to hurry. When I got to the top of the Crack, A. found something had gone wrong with the film, so I had to do it all over again. Again whilst doing the top block, we were driven up at

Siegfried Herford (following) on the Mantelshelf, Scafell Pinnacle

such a rate that both of us felt in danger of tumbling off. However, we did it. After this strenuous effort, we went up the Abbey Ridge with Thomson and down the West Chimney. [3]

It was a far cry from his boyhood ascent of the Needle when he got back to Keswick with a wonderful sense of triumph; now it was all in a day's work.

On November 2nd of the same year, Siegfried attended the first Annual Dinner as a fully- fledged Club member, the Club's sixth dinner, held at the Sun Hotel, Coniston, the Club's Lakeland headquarters. By the sound of it he thoroughly enjoyed himself. May was again back at Oxford, and he sent her a comprehensive account of the event:

> The chief event of the past fortnight for me has been the visit to Coniston for the Fell and Rock Dinner. I went up on the Friday night as far as Barrow, where I was put up for the night by a climbing friend. The next morning I and a number of other Rockfellers went on to Coniston. The Sun Hotel at Coniston only holds about 20 people and as over 100 people come up for the Dinner the remainder have to be boarded out all over the village. After we had succeeded in finding our respective rooms and had changed, we wandered up to Doe Crags. I was climbing that day with a rather nervous and timid man, a school-master; I therefore chose the severest thing on the rocks as a suitable object of attack. I am afraid I kept him waiting nearly one hour in one place, and as it was rather cold, he was not in a happy frame of mind when the time came for him to follow. However, I cheered him up by reminding him of the big drop there was, and also with prospects of the Dinner in the evening, so at length he managed to get up; I believe his waist felt rather sore before he had finished, but all such discomforts were but an additional glory when in the evening, replete, and with cigar in mouth, his valiant efforts thrilled for the n-th time the awe inspired females in his vicinity. I myself was well situated at the Dinner with pleasant people all round, and was in a very amiable frame of mind by the end of the evening, as indeed was everybody else. There were many speeches; probably the best was that of Margery Eckward, who represented the Ladies Scottish Climbing Club. Among others who spoke were Prof. Collingwood of Coniston, and C.T. Needham M.P., who indulged in platitude about mountain beauty. On the following day, Sunday, Laycock and I had the honour of conducting Haskett Smith, the new President of

the Club, up some climbs on Doe Crags. He is of course the Chief Pioneer of Lakeland climbing, but is getting on in years now. He is a very cheery old boy, and regales you with anecdotes all the way up a climb. Most of the climbers returned from Coniston that evening at 6.30. We got into Manchester at 1.30., and I walked home with M. Eckward from Chorlton, getting in about 2.30.

In addition to Siegfried's letter, there is a photograph of the Fell and Rock group at Goat's Water, a pleasant memento of the sixth Dinner. The letter does not specify what Siegfried climbed with Haskett Smith, but we do know that Siegfried added the 'Very Difficult' Falcon Variation to D.Buttress. Although Siegfried was only 20 at the time, and thus very much a member of the younger squad, the Club already recognised his special status by asking him to take care of their distinguished new President. It would be interesting to know whether Siegfried took his chance to take on the 'cheery old boy' (who once clung in desperation to a ledge muttering an appropriate line from Homer in the original Greek) and challenge his derogatory assessment of Plynlimon. Plynlimon, one of the Herford family's favourite mountains back in the Aberystwyth days, had been rudely dismissed as 'neither easy to see nor worth looking at when seen'. The Professor would have given the Great Man a long, hard stare!

Margery Eckward, whom Siegfried thought probably made the best speech of the evening, was a neighbour of the Herfords at Didsbury. Her home was Broome House, a large, rambling building on the main road, now a residential provision for children in the care of Manchester Social Services. It is not clear when the two first met, but they knew each other well before the Fell and Rock dinner, for Siegfried recorded that they had climbed together at Wharncliffe and Cratcliffe Tor in 1910. She was to become the only woman member of his tight inner climbing circle.

From a climbing point of view, there is every reason why they might have met, for Margery Eckward was an able climber, experienced at handling the Scottish peaks, which is why she became a member of the Ladies Scottish Climbing Club in 1908, shortly after the Club's formation, hardly a bunch of shrinking violets. She also knew her way around the Alps. During the summer prior to the Dinner, she had been doing some stiff climbing in the Dolomites, in the company of Miss Inglis Clark, sister to Charles Inglis Clark, who, like Siegfried, became a victim of the First World War, and whose life is commemorated by the hut in the Allt a'Mhuilinn on Ben Nevis. This doughty *cordée feminine* achieved two new routes on La Pizza. There is a letter she wrote to Marie Herford, dated 1920 or 1921, in which she described a much earlier day on Wharncliffe. They had been joined by C.E.Montague, author of the masterful *Hanging Garden Gully* and other notable short stories, a close family friend of the Herfords, and like them, an ardent supporter of Lady Barn House.

Siegfried was sitting on a boulder and his hair was blowing in the wind and I felt about him just as Mr Young felt when he met him that day on the Welsh hill top. He had the perfect unselfconsciousness of a child. I remember thinking how much I should like to have a boy like that. You must be very proud to have had Siegfried.

It was unquestionably a thoughtful and kind thing to have said to his mother, but just how unselfconscious a child he was is more open to question – the sort of image well served to perpetuate a legend. Laycock, who had suffered from time to time under his temperament, and his all too consciously worked-out self-image, the Guardian image if you like, might well have thought he detected a feminine – a mothering – susceptibility to his charm. There was no other type of susceptibility. The year following the Dinner, Margery Eckward married Philip Waterlow, which caused her to move to Hampstead in London. Siegfried remained in close touch. After his own move south, to the Royal Aircraft Factory at Farnborough, he spent several weekends with the Waterlows, sometimes attending meetings or concerts. Eventually, after her family came along, she gave up climbing completely, resigning from the Ladies Scottish Climbing Club in 1924.

Siegfried was now on overdrive. On April 12th, 1912, he and Sansom made the first ascent of Kern Knotts West Buttress, and he followed this, with W.B.Brunskill, by making the first descent of the Eagle's Nest Ridge. It was all rather breathless. He had reached a stage of stamina and fitness which enabled him to keep going without a hint of fatigue. C.F.Holland, no sluggard himself, remembered his amazing energy on the North-West Climb on Pillar. Siegfried had led George Abraham and Holland up the climb. When they reached the top, a fourth climber appeared who said that he had never been up the North-West, so Siegfried immediately went down with him and repeated the climb. Nor was that the last of it. On the same day, when the group were having tea at Burnthwaite, he suddenly remarked that Holland had never done Kern Knotts Crack. The two of them rushed off to do the climb there and then, only just coming out the better in a race against fading light.

Ruskin compared mountains to cathedrals, and if the comparison is sound (Siegfried would have rejected it), then Siegfried was hardly ever off his knees before the shrine during the precocious season of 1912. Mentally and physically he gave himself over to what Laycock in Skye had called

George Sansom leading John Laycock on the first ascent of Kern Knotts West Buttress, April 12th 1912

the religion, equipped and strengthened by constant worship in the rarefied cathedral air. He was creating his own standard as he went along. He did not deliberately rebel against the traditions of his contemporaries, but imperceptibly they no longer influenced him, and he refused to be bound. Occasionally, again without intending to, he found himself having a brush with the High Priests of the Faith. On one occasion the High Priest turned out to be William T. Palmer, an original member of the Fell and Rock, prolific writer on all matters affecting Cumberland, and at the time editor of the Club's Journal. Somehow, in his tweed jacket and 'pendulous' plus-fours, he seemed to represent an older generation. He was to give Siegfried a ticking off. Siegfried was climbing Kern Knotts Crack when he noticed that the first chockstone, then used for swinging out of the 'Niche', was about to be dislodged, so he removed it completely. Reporting what he had done in the Journal, he facetiously remarked that the chockstone could be had on application at the Wastwater Hotel. Righteous paroxysms followed: 'The Editor wonders', declared Palmer, 'if S.W.H. has read the article "Excitement at Wasdalehead" in No.4 – the crime of altering climbs as there dealt with, is a serious one'. It is an odd censure from a member of a generation who spent their time altering climbs by way of endless gardening. [4]

The more one thinks about what Siegfried did in the Lake District, his attitude and approach to climbing, the more one has to say he seemed to be preparing himself for the great climbs ahead of him. 'Where the rainbow ends', runs the old folk-saying, 'lies a crock of gold'. Even during the youthful family holidays he appeared to be seeking the crock of gold; on Napes Needle, defining his ambition and self-imposed expectations. 'I have been up Napes Needle, that's all' would one day become 'I have been up Scafell Crag, that's all'. He had found the end of the rainbow. There is no record to show exactly when he first climbed on Scafell Crag, what he did or who was with him, but we do know that by the time of his election to the Fell and Rock, Siegfried and the vast, brooding mass of rock had become indivisible, the intractable granite riveted in his soul, commanding him to embrace Destiny and climb as a prophet climbs. [5]

The first of the great climbs took place on April 17th, 1912 – the Direct from Lord's Rake to Hopkinson's Cairn, partnered by George Sansom, although others were also around, particularly W.B. Brunskill.

Siegfried's audacious lead of the Direct from Lord's Rake has to be seen against the background of the fate of a previous party to attempt the climb. On a cold and blustery day, in the September of 1903, a terrible accident occurred on the face of the Pinnacle, the worst catastrophe to afflict British climbing since the ill-fated triumph of Edward Whymper on the Matterhorn back in 1865, and like that dramatic event, the Scafell accident claimed four lives. The bodies of R.W. Broadrick, A.E.W. Garrett, Henry Jupp and Stanley Ridsdale, were discovered spread out on the scree below the climb. It was a terrible sight, one which covered the Pinnacle with an aura of doom, and had the serious impact of setting Lakeland climbing back by several years. It was with this knowledge that Siegfried prepared for his assault on the Direct from Lord's Rake, a challenge no less psychological than it was technical, feeling that the time had come to exorcise the spell of doom.

In the group who watched Siegfried tackle the climb was W.B. Brunskill, an able rock-climber himself, the man who had partnered Siegfried on the second ascent of Jones's Route. Sansom said that he found Brunskill 'a delightful man in every way', despite him being strange, sometimes to the point of eccentricity, a strict vegetarian who wore the minimum of clothes even in bitterly cold weather, and who always climbed in bare feet. A man of ultra-strong opinions, which he would express forcibly, he had been elected to the Fell and Rock in 1909, but resigned from the Club prematurely over a matter which never developed into an issue. He is remembered now more for photographs than his climbs, for he was a photographer of brilliance, an artist with the camera, taking some of the best pictures of Siegfried in action, and doing so by capturing the texture of the rock, together with the feel of Edwardian days. His obituarist said that he disposed of his negatives, which presumably means he destroyed them – a serious loss.

Brunskill wrote an account of Siegfried on the Direct from Lord's Rake which he entitled *The Finest Rock Climb in England*. [6] He settled to his task with a flourish:

> In remotest Lakeland there stands a lofty tower of the firmest clean-cut rock. Six hundred feet is the height of it. Its pediment measures many yards across. And from its foundations start masses of steeply sloping slabs which sweep upwards into the vertical. As one stands below and gazes up, it seems to resemble some fantastic temple reared with buttresses and spiral stairways, which dwindle to nothing on the distant skyline. It is the Pinnacle Rock of Scafell. So far we have seen that the only way to climb the tower direct from its base, was to circumvent the difficulties below the halfway ledge by making an exit to the easier rock above the toe traverse. Jones had thought in the dim light of that Easter evening a way looked feasible. [7] Later explorers had abandoned it; for the long upper slab below

Scafell Pinnacle   Photo: Abraham Bros

George Sansom and Herford on The Gangway, Jones's Route – note the stockinged feet

the Cairn seemed hopeless. That an attempt has been made upon it by the 1903 party was evident from many nail-marks at its foot. Throughout the length of its long flat surface there is but one resting place – a long pull up from the narrow ledge below; above it a tiny hold, the length and width of a finger. After this is the mauvais pas, a tremendous stretch to the crack which bounds the slab on the right by the side of an overhanging nose, and thence upwards by the almost holdless crack. This is the thrilling piece of work Jones mentions.

Soon after Easter this year a climber, young but experienced in many ascents, started alone from Lord' s Rake. His boots are left below, and soon he is passing silently from the Gangway out on to the broad face beyond. With skilled eye he scans the rock, searching out every hold around, and seeming to make swift mental trial of each, before he makes an upward movement, lightly and without apparent effort. It is a weird exhibition of the cat-like.

To his companions, watching from below, it is but a short time till he comes to the final difficulty. From some tiny holds, an arm-pull and a neat press-up bring his feet to the safe hold. He must next project himself against the rock (it is rough and slopes back a little) until he can rise on the finger ledge, and get upon it. It is done, and he is ready for the stretch across. A second or so for breath, and he swings over to the crack, and slowly hand over hand, goes up. Good holds are waiting for him at the top, and the next moment he is by the Cairn. A coil of rope is lying there. He drops an end into Deep Ghyll, hauls up his boots; and then a companion, safe-guarded by the rope, follows up the way he has come. Thence they climb on together. Holds are now numerous, and spikes for belaying, until the rock slopes away, and they pass out along a narrow ridge to the summit.

So ends this latest phase of the climbing on Scafell Pinnacle. For twenty-five years it has awaited completion; and even now, though the conquest has been made, there are no nail-marks to point out the route for others, who will be coming soon to try the way. There is but the Cairn, away up the face of this finest of climbs, a fitting memorial of those who here and elsewhere have met their end in the mischances which fate is ever dealing out to the skilled and unskilled alike.

Brunskill's account is highly revealing. Hitherto, it has always been taken for granted that Siegfried was seconded by Sansom all the way up, but according to Brunskill, Siegfried soloed unroped as far as what is now Herford's Slab and the Cairn, and only then brought Sansom up to him, finishing off together. It was a concentrated piece of exposed climbing. It is often unwise to compare climbs, but while the Direct from Lord's Rake is undoubtedly less technically demanding than Central Buttress, it might be argued that it was the more daring lead of the two, for not only had Siegfried to overcome the integral difficulties, he had also to exorcise an aura of death then permeating the climb. There is also the point that he was two years older and more experienced on Central Buttress. However, whether it was the more daring lead of the two or not, Brunskill himself came away with a grizzly reminder of the 1903 debacle:

> Here, by the writer, lies a boot-heel, with half its climbing nails torn out. On the under side a deep gash runs across it. It was found tightly wedged in the trough where Hopkinson's party were stopped by the ice [8] and from this it is likely that its owner, climbing last in his turn from the trough, and hearing a slip high above, jumped back, but too late, and was jerked from it far out onto the scree two hundred feet beneath.

Siegfried and Sansom were not yet finished that year with the name of Hopkinson. On June 19th, they were back at the foot of the Pinnacle, only this time it was the first ascent of Hopkinson's Gully that they were after, a Severe climb that was to give Sansom so much pleasure over the years, and to which he regularly returned.

There are many entries by Siegfried and Sansom, together with others who climbed with them, in the Wasdale Hotel Climbing Book 1863-1919. One entry recorded the Girdle Traverse of Scafell, bringing to maturity an idea first worked out on Castle Naze. The Girdle was one of Sansom's cunningly devised plans, spearheaded on the crag by Siegfried, the zoologist's stalking instinct made to work by the engineer. The plan involved 1,100 feet of continuous climbing, starting at the first pitch of Professor's Chimney on the right of the crag and finishing up on the left at the top of Collier's Climb. On September 12th, 1912, they trudged up Brown Tongue under the optimistic illusion that one day would be enough for the climb, but in fact they did not complete it until the 14th. Siegfried was under some pressure about time, because by then, having received his Degree at the School of Engineering, he was due at the Royal Aircraft Factory at Farnborough where his research scholarship needed attending to.

On the day of the climb they were surprised to bump into Brunskill and

H.B. Gibson. As both were eager to join forces, it was a party of four which set off.

The start was not encouraging, in a moss-covered, slimy, Deep Ghyll, and it took about all Siegfried could do to stay on the rock. They crossed the Pinnacle Face, which Siegfried found one of the most delightful sections of the entire Girdle, and, because of their previous knowledge of the place, they moved fast with their boots off. Pisgah Buttress did not confront them with the problems they thought it might, a near horizontal ledge taking them directly to the Fives Court, from where they used the usual route for a descent into Moss Ghyll. Once again previous exploration paid off at the unclimbed Central Buttress, towering above them, and a beautiful traverse took them into a furrow, providing access to a thin line across Central Buttress. Siegfried was impressed by the position:

> The ledge on which we now stood is in many ways unique, and is certainly one of the most remarkable places in Cumberland. Above it, the wall of the Central Buttress rises sheer for several hundred feet, almost hopelessly smooth and steep, while there is a sufficiently precipitous drop down Rake's Progress to make one move circumspectly. At the further end of the ledge Botterill's Slab shows its full height and looks appallingly difficult.

They were now in fact at the Oval, a name enshrined in the history of Scafell, and so christened owing to Sansom's addiction to cricket. But it was now late, and had started to get dark, so after using Moss Ghyll for a tactical withdrawal, they shot down to the valley and the hotel.

The 13th dawned wet, stayed wet all day, so nothing got done, in marked contrast to a gloriously fine morning on the 14th, when they were back on the rock by eight o'clock. Instead of pressing on, moving left from the Oval as they originally intended to do, they traversed across the upper section of Central Buttress, a *cul de sac* of some difficulty, and then they wasted a lot of time on the Bayonet-shaped Crack area, where Siegfried rounded a sensational corner on doubtful holds. It turned out a time-consuming and fruitless manoeuvre and they were forced back to the point they had vacated two days previously. They got themselves to a ledge some 30 feet below the Oval, a tricky and exposed situation with much gardening to be done, but confidence grew once Gibson unearthed a solid belay, and they quickly got themselves to the foot of Botterill's Slab. Siegfried knew the Slab, having led Brunskill on the second ascent of it, and as darkness was again fast approaching, they sent a man to the top of the Keswick Brother's Climb from where a safeguarding rope could be lowered. The stratagem worked

George Sansom

C F Holland belayed at the foot of the Bayonet-shaped Crack on the first ascent of Central Buttress, Scafell

nicely and they finished up the left wall of the recess in which lies the final section of Collier's Climb. It had turned out a magnificent climb. Most climbers nowadays finish the Girdle at the top of Botterill's Slab, which would have interested Siegfried, for he was of the view that Botterill's would prevent the Girdle from becoming popular. Standards and expectations change.

In the evening, two days later, sitting in front of the fire at his digs, 72 Peabody Road, South Farnborough, Siegfried could read a report of his exploits in *The Manchester Guardian* (December 16th, 1912), where the Girdle Traverse was described as 'the most exacting climb in Great Britain'. He could also tell Margery Eckward about his climbs when he stayed at Hampstead. On one occasion they attended a Bradlaugh Society Dinner at the Holborn Restaurant, with Bernard Shaw in the Chair:

> There were all sorts of queer looking people there, as you might imagine (he wrote to May), most of them being shaggy-headed atheists with flaming red ties, a number of women, most of them of elephantine proportions, looking more like innkeepers' wives than intelligent rationalists, and a small sprinkling of respectable looking people like ourselves. Bernard Shaw made a very witty speech; he referred to Bradlaugh as a man who got more intoxi - cated from a glass of water than an ordinary person would from ten barrels of boiling brandy! Mrs Bradlaugh Bomer (Bradlaugh's daughter) also spoke, dropping most of her h's which got on my nerves horribly – Altogether, we spent an amusing evening.

His phrase, 'looking more like innkeepers' wives', carries with it an echo of the disdain he reserved for 'what you might imagine of country people'. He was still Lietz's Guardian, conventional, working through the mainstream, 'basking in a canoe on the pond' at Sansom's house at Godalming. The mountains were seldom out of his mind. He would take a hurried few days for a Fell and Rock meet, like the one in February, 1913, when the crags were plastered with ice and he and Laycock contented themselves with an old-fashioned round of the Old Man. As he worked at Farnborough, probing the intricacies of aeronautics, the consciousness of the unclimbed Central Buttress kept coming to him.

CHAPTER TEN

TWO FRIENDSHIPS

'Nothing discovers or cements friendship more quickly', wrote Geoffrey Winthrop Young, 'than common action or adventure shared'. It was both common action and adventure shared which first brought Siegfried into contact with the omnipresent Laycock, and Winthrop Young himself. Laycock and Young were as different as chalk and cheese, in their sociability, their mannerisms and style, in intellectual sharpness, and in the type of climbing which attracted them. They were both strong characters, Laycock a lawyer and politician, Young an educationalist and poet, and they came within Siegfried's orbit at different stages of his development, each acting as a catalyst that would propel him forward. Each man found that Siegfried aroused strong emotions in them, and all that was discovered or cemented along the way remains an open question.

Given the large amount of time Siegfried spent climbing, it is no surprise that both Laycock and Young first came across him in a mountain setting, Laycock in the gaunt ravine of Kinder Downfall, Young on a wintry summit of Tryfan.

It is a pity that we do not have Siegfried's own account of his meeting with Winthrop Young or any indication of what he was doing on his own among the Welsh mountains. Had it not been for Winthrop Young, we would not have known he was there. Young, by contrast, wrote two versions of the encounter, one in an unpublished letter of poignant spontaneity which he sent to the Professor (February 15th, 1916), shortly after Siegfried's death, and the other in *Mountains with a Difference*, published almost fifty years after the event. [1]

> *The Letter.* I met your boy first on the peak of Tryfan. I was alone, and the strange figure, tattered, with great blue eyes and wind-tossed shock of hair, came up the other side, and joined me, in silence, looking into our valley. I had heard of him in the region, and guessed who he must be. It was like meeting a spirit of the hills. I think all I said was: 'Won't you come over and join us at Pen y Pass?' And he just came, without saying anything or seeming to think it necessary to leave word or bring 'things'.
>
> And so he remained for me always: a strange, aloof, extraordinarily sympathetic appearance coming suddenly at intervals and disappear-

ing, in London or elsewhere. Sometimes he would sit in the same chair a whole day and talk the light round. Sometimes he hardly spoke, but just came round on my walks with me, in the best companionship of silence. I have never known a more simple, clear mind, or a character of greater independence and charm. It was always like a breath of clean wind, wind that came in sunlight. Without a touch of affectation or other-worldliness he had an atmosphere of thought and personality with him for which I can find no word but purity, but it is not one which gives a right impression. There was a firmness of will and decision of a well-reasoned mind, combined with the rare remoteness, detachment, untouchableness of a singularly sympathetic childhood.

I felt that he trusted.

To me he embodied all that I most cherished, and hoped for, in the world of mountaineering, and open winds. He was the future, as I liked to think it would continue and develop in him. The finest tradition of mountain inspiration, knowledge, and feeling, in a body of unequalled power. That he was the greatest rock climber of all time is only a part. He was to me far more, the essence, almost the spirit of the great spaces, clear lines and lasting inspiration of the mountains themselves. A son of sunlight, movement, and the great elemental forces that are remote from passion and small things.

The account of the meeting in *Mountains with a Difference* is more controlled and condensed, with some added detail – that Tryfan was snow covered and that Winthrop Young had reached the top of the mountain by way of a scramble up the east face. When he reached the summit, just as a red sun was sinking behind the Nant Ffrancon, he came across a 'sturdy and tattered figure with a shock of strong flaxen hair'. The invitation for Siegfried to join the Pen-y-Pass party, together with his silent response, is repeated, but the real interest lies with added detail which came after. As in the letter, Winthrop Young referred to Siegfried's visits to him in London, but this time, instead of walks 'in the best companionship of silence', we are told how they attended concerts together, and, more unexpectedly, called in at various London boxing rings.

The moving and heartfelt letter is suffused with the euphony of a poet, one of the few genuine poets of the hills, and it abounds with honest emotion. Winthrop told the Herfords how Siegfried 'embodied all that I most cherished, and hoped for, in the world of mountaineering, and open winds'. He believed that Siegfried was one of the three young men who epitomised all the highest ideals of the past and the brightest hope for the future. Earlier he had singled out Hugh Rose Pope, before Pope's fatal fall in the Pyrenees, with 'his unique power, wrestling up against the flood'; and he would subsequently do so with George Mallory, 'that magnificent courage and endurance, that joyous and supreme triumph of human spirit over all circumstances'. It was illustrious company for Siegfried to find himself in.

Laycock's obituary of Siegfried in the 1916 *Fell and Rock Climbing Club Journal*, seems almost staid alongside Winthrop Young's writing, but it was a wonderful piece of self-control. It covers up how Laycock's sense of loss was almost total. Other than Stanley Jeffcoat, he had known Siegfried longer than any other climber, and he had been out on the hills with him more often even than Sansom. There is no sign in the obituary that the poor man went to pieces when the news of Siegfried's death reached him. Laycock had served right through the war, holding the rank of 2nd Lieutenant, and although he had frequently been in the thick of the fighting, he was one of the lucky ones who came through. Like others of his generation, he had seen much of death, and like them, he had to make what sense of it he could. Siegfried's death cut him to pieces, his entire world collapsed, and all that had made life intelligible to him – *the* religion – had gone. He was to be haunted by the spectre of loss for the rest of his days. He did try to climb again, but it was no use, empty without Siegfried, and, giving up climbing altogether, he fled the country for good. Laycock escaped to Singapore, where, in 1920, he was called to the Singapore Bar; then later, as leader of the Progressive Party, he found himself elected the first European member of the Legislative Assembly. Despite these successes, his heart was broken, and he died in Singapore in December 1960, aged 73, far from the heroic deeds and voices of home. He ended, after all, one further victim of the Great War.

Laycock's well-worked Journal Obituary did not convey how he really felt. He was much more open in a letter he sent to the Professor and Marie Herford (March, 1916): 'For many years', he confessed 'he has been my dearest friend, and a great deal more'. He did not enlarge on 'a great deal more', but the letter, coupled with his emotional turmoil, suggest that, from his side at least, there was a distinct psycho-sexual element in his dealings with Siegfried.

With Winthrop Young a homosexual dimension was never to be ruled out. His biographer has appraised us of the full extent of his active homosexual life.[2] He began as a boy at Marlborough College, and, by the time he was teaching at Eton, he had become highly experienced. There was trouble at Eton, and he was sacked. 'Exceptional circumstances' was the euphemism used at the time by the Provost and Fellows, and while we are not told in so many words that he was caught *in flagrante*, we are left to guess. Later on, in similar fashion, he was compelled to resign prematurely from the Schools Inspectorate.

Winthrop Young would by no means have been alone in his misfortune; the ruined schoolmaster appeared on the scene with monotonous pertinacity. Siegfried would have known for himself that throughout the public school sector there was a tacit acceptance of a homosexual ethos. Much of it was constrained. What was true of Marlborough and Eton was replicated at Boxgrove and the Hermann Lietz-Schule. The male bonding, the almost mystic, manly ideal, was bound up with a deep admiration for the heyday of Greek civilisation. The injunction, 'Quit you like Men', when used at a public school, had more in common with the ideals of brave sacrifice on the battlefield which characterised the lovers who made up the Spartan and Theban armies, than it had with goings-on in Fitzrovia.

When Siegfried sat in Young's London rooms, when sometimes he talked and at others hardly spoke a word, he must have been fully aware of the risks his friend took. A widespread homophobia in society at large resulted in cruel and illiberal laws. The risk was not so much a question of offending an hypocritical rectitude, as landing up in court on a charge of indecency, the very charge which sent Oscar Wilde to prison. His trial took place in Siegfried's lifetime, with its impact still felt, sending the forbidden *cognoscenti* scurrying off to their burrows. (There is a delicious irony about the Wilde trial. The Rt. Hon. Alfred Wills, Judge of Queen's Bench, passed sentence with the words: 'Oscar Wilde, the crime of which you have been convicted is so bad that one has to put stern restraint upon one's self to prevent one's self from describing, in language which I would rather not use, the sentiments which must rise to the breast of every man of honour'. It is difficult to imagine how a mountaineer of distinction could allow himself to say anything so fatuous. Wills was the third President of the Alpine Club, author of *Wanderings among the High Alps*, and it was his ascent of the Wetterhorn in 1854 which is said to have ushered in the 'Golden Age' of mountaineering. The irony is that, five years after sending Wilde down, it was Wills himself who proposed Winthrop Young, the arch-homosexual, for membership to the Alpine Club.) Young's association with Wills – by itself would have alerted him to the dangers. Everyone knew the score. Lytton Strachey's ecstatic 'Mon Dieu!' letter, addressed to Clive and Vanessa Bell, describing how his hand trembled and heart palpitated at the breathtaking beauty of George Mallory, has been famously quoted. Maynard Keynes, at Cambridge, gave him a warning:

There is no risk so long as no-one has anything to do with the lower classes, or people off the streets.

Winthrop Young had no such qualms. He might be in Soho, or disappear for the weekend to the homosexual subculture of Berlin or Paris, riotous parties, orgiastic frenzies, escapes and pick-ups. Young was prepared for risks, as he was at Eton, and he took his chances.

The mystery in all this is what induced Siegfried to go along with Young on his visits to dingy and insalubrious boxing booths. There was much to attract Young; a love of physical movement, whether climbing, dancing, or boxing; the sheer vitality of swaying young men dodging about, jabbing and jerking, glinting with sweat. It was sexually arousing in a troubadour atmosphere, with the excitement of the unexpected, getting caught up in a brawl, finding yourself cornered by young toughies who knew their price, or the worst outcome of all, finding yourself apprehended by the authorities in the company of a young man. What was Siegfried doing in such places? It is pretty certain he never wrote to his parents or to May describing these sorties as he did his visit to the Bradlaugh Society. For Young, boxing, or his predatory prowls, was all part of the vitality of living, but for Siegfried it meant a Guardian mingling with the lower classes as one of them, people he had dismissed as peasants back at Schloss Bieberstein.

There could be a simple but interesting explanation. What drew him into 'slumming', the world of the cheap boxing booth, was the lure of adventure. Really, he knew nothing about the seedy side of life, what destitute people got up to in their ghettos, and in this sense the boxing booths acted as an adventure into the unknown, the world of the homeless and unfed drunkards, the criminals and harlots. If this is the explanation, and it was a lure of adventure which motivated him, then he followed an outstanding precedent. In a long since forgotten book, *A Tramp to Brighton*, the great mountaineer Edward Shirley Kennedy, 'father of the Alpine Club' and President before Alfred Wills, explained how he came to take up his important philanthropic work in the East End of London.[3] Kennedy, a devout Christian, accepted the invitation of a philanthropist friend to accompany him into the slums simply because it sounded an adventurous thing to do. He went, not in the 'hope of benefiting the criminal classes', as he put it, but because the element of danger appealed to him in exactly the same sense that it did in the mountains. He was not ready for what he found; he was appalled. Kennedy stayed on, sometimes living rough alongside his 'thieves and slashers', using his influence and enormous wealth to help set up an organisation which instigated pioneering support work for discharged prisoners, an institution that, under a different guise, continues to this day.[4]

We have to accept that there was, or seems to have been, a lecherous impulse to Winthrop Young, something completely lacking in John Laycock. Despite a reputation for being combative, Laycock was a sociable character on the surface, but because he was well capable of covering over his true feelings, one can never be sure about what really drove him. Both men, in their different ways, had an integrity of feeling when it came to Siegfried, and there was a great deal at stake for all three of them. It is perhaps a fair summary to say that their friendship was rooted in common action and adventure shared. Winthrop Young came to exert the more dominant influence during the final three years of Siegfried's life. It must have been an absorbing attraction, almost inspirational, for Young to have encountered on the summit of Tryfan a flaxen-haired, German-looking youth, already a climber of exceptional ability, a self-confessed Guardian and willing disciple of Lietz. The young man was the embodiment of alluring qualities Young was bound to find irresistible. For whatever else Winthrop Young may or may not have been, he was an outstanding mountaineer of greatness, a poet of evocative flowering, and an educationalist, if not of vision, then of originality who knew all about Lietz. He was perceptive enough to single out two of Siegfried's fundamental characteristics, a well-reasoned mind coupled with a body of unequalled power – the two mighty forces he was compelled to grapple with as a boy, not always with success.

Siegfried followed Winthrop Young down from the summit of Tryfan, joining the Pen-y -Pass party, going out climbing with that 'knight of chivalry', George Mallory. Young painted an enduring picture of the three of them, traversing together the sweeping precipices of Lliwedd:

> There followed a frosty day of sun; when he and Mallory and I started up the far east cracks of Lliwedd and then swept athwart the whole snow-covered face of the precipices, making the second Girdle traverse. We were roped, for the rock was ice-fronded and snow-flecked. We climbed very fast.

It is a lasting image of the 'master of the starry way' capturing a snow-stolen moment with the flower of Edwardian youth. At the hue of dusk, they returned to the warm solidity of Pen-y-Pass, with its steam baths and cultured talk and noisy games in the smoke-room, parties that had nurtured two generations of talented climbers, and now tinged with the elegant wistfulness of a caste vaguely aware that its authority was on the wane.

CHAPTER ELEVEN

CENTRAL BUTTRESS

The Herford legend is founded on the hallowed rock of the Central Buttress of Scafell, on historic events which took place there, how Siegfried and Sansom took on a sensational enterprise and won through. George Sansom's account of the ascent in the 1914 *Fell and Rock Climbing Club Journal* is a recognised and much quoted classic, and while no man could have been luckier with his chronicler, it is a document that has helped to perpetuate the myth: 'He who makes the true ascent', said Saint Gregory of Nyssa, 'must ascend for ever'.

Time has its corrosive way with reputations, true of Central Buttress as with everything else, and although the climb is still regarded as a serious undertaking, it is no longer the unknown, the intimidating challenge it proved for Siegfried and his companions. This is the point Geoff Oliver had in mind when he wrote:

> No longer the ultimate test for the tiger, it is now a trade route within the capabilities of numerous climbers, a fact that often leads to a queue at the Oval. Many an unfortunate wretch has struggled on the Flake Crack to the accompaniment of derisory banter from the impatient watchers below. [1]

The thought of a queue at the Oval would have delighted Siegfried as much as it would have surprised and staggered him. He would have taken heart by the way that the capabilities of numerous climbers represent an enormous jump in technical standard. Yet, at the same time, how many of the young climbers acknowledge in their turn that their struggles on Flake Crack are a measure of the lasting impact Siegfried's climb made, the influence the climb has exerted over the years, acting as a catalyst for progress? The point is well made by Kelly and Doughty:

> Undoubtedly it stamped climbing with yet a new hallmark, and the inspiration due to it is not yet exhausted: all the great modern climbs in the British Isles are its lineal descendants. [2]

In the same way, the impatient watchers bantering at the Oval are Siegfried's lineal descendants, each bringing to the experience of being on the climb their own personal angle of vision, yet also in a sense waiting their turn to retrace a little bit of climbing history.

The guide book says that Central Buttress was first climbed on April

Jeffcoat's
Ledge.

The Great
Flake.

Flake Crack.

The Oval.

Slab Start.

Central Buttress
Scafell.

Richard J. 1995

20th- 22nd, 1914. That is true as far as it goes, for that was when the climb was finally mastered, but the dates were the outcome of a protracted campaign. We do not know when Siegfried first turned his gaze on Central Buttress, when the lure of the great sweep of rock entered his bones, but we do know that the contest proved a long drawn out affair, covering a period of at least two years, and that during the battle siege tactics were brought into play more reminiscent of the great faces of the Alps than the lesser ranges of home. In that sense, as with others, Central Buttress is a distinctly modern climb.

Sansom's account opened in mid-June 1912, when Siegfried and himself, feeling in an inquisitive frame of mind, climbed up a grassy scoop leading out of Moss Ghyll on to the Central Buttress:

> We did not seriously believe that we should find a new climb on this rock face, for it appears to be singularly unbroken and almost vertical for over 200 ft. It was however an unknown region and as such appealed to us. The scoop was not very difficult and we were soon looking round a corner at the top along a narrow grassy ledge which apparently extended right across the face to Botterill's Slab. The rocks fell away very steeply below and a sheer smooth wall rose up to a great height above. Its regularity was interrupted at one point, it is true, by an enormous rock flake which tapered out to nothing, 70 ft higher.

The two of them continued with their probe, but the climbing became more awkward, suggesting that further progress scarcely seemed feasible, so they called it a day and switched over to Pisgah Buttress and climbed that instead. However, despite their feelings of frustration, the probe turned out highly profitable, as it demonstrated the possibility of reaching Botterill's Slab from Moss Ghyll, thus providing the key to a Girdle Traverse. Three months later, in the September, Siegfried led the second ascent of Botterill's and the Girdle was completed.

The first sighting of the notorious Flake Crack disquieted Sansom and he came away convinced that Central Buttress would not go. It was a depressing outcome Siegfried did not share. Siegfried was altogether more aggressive in his reaction to what had been seen. Following the successful completion of the Girdle Traverse, and his return to Didsbury, he wrote a letter to Sansom who was down at Godalming:

> The whole idea and credit of the G.T. are due to you, to whom all thanks are due. At your request I have put together a short article (8 or 9 pp) and have sent it to Palmer; I hope he will accept it. [He

did. See *Fell and Rock Journal*, 1912] If you wish to see it now I can send you a copy, but I am thinking the Journal will seem rather fresher to you when it comes out if you are not already familiar with half of its contents. Yes, we must look at the C.B. again; I have not yet given up hope. That overhanging Flake must be tried.

It was a justified tribute to Sansom, the mastermind behind the Girdle, although he was honest enough to admit that he could not have led it. Meanwhile, as the letter makes clear, Siegfried was already mulling over in his mind how to tackle the Flake. (Have we, in this hitherto unpublished letter, the first time-honoured reference to Central Buttress as C.B.?)

There was no further activity until the June and July of the following year, 1913.

In the June, Siegfried and Sansom found themselves back at the Oval, now the muster point for attack, the objective being nothing less than the Flake itself. The first to lead off was Sansom. His first task was to struggle with a narrow crack, which according to him was 30 ft above the Oval, 40 ft in length, and, he estimated that the top overhung the bottom by some 12 feet. The distances he gave do not correspond with those in the modern guide book, where the section from the Oval to the end of the Flake is divided into three pitches with a total distance of 65 feet. The pitch gave him a desperate struggle but in the end he managed to reach a large bulge in the side of the Flake, where he took a good look at the crack which followed, and doubting whether it would go, he settled for a retreat. At this point, Siegfried took over the lead, only this time getting a little further, gingerly pressing upward until he managed to negotiate the bulge and thereby giving himself a good view of the problem ahead. That is as far as the push went. Once again, boldness was mingled with prudence, for he had decided that it was unjustifiable to go on without a better knowledge of what lay in store. The end of the second probe marked an interruption for Sansom, who sailed for the forests of Brazil on a zoological expedition, in search of animals as little known as the Flake itself.

During the period Sansom was away, in the July, there occurred what he himself described as 'probably one of the most remarkable and bold explorations ever carried out in the district'. He was able to sit in Brazil and learn the details from a well-known letter sent to him by Siegfried.[3] To some extent we shall have to rely on the letter, but in the hope of adding to the history of the climb, we shall quote instead an unpublished letter Siegfried wrote to Brunskill a week after he had written to Sansom. Headed 'Wales', and dated July 22nd, he wrote:

I meant to have written to you before going up to Wasdale, but somehow or other forgot to, so I must rest content with telling you of our doings. I was up there for a fortnight, J.L. (John Laycock) for a week, Jeffcoat for 10 days, but J.L. was in bad form and did hardly any climbing. We did all the usuals on the Napes, E.M., etc. also K.K.W.B. *[Kern Knotts West Buttress]*, which we *descended*. Another day, we did the direct finish to Woodhead's, going straight up from top of 2nd pitch; it is not very hard, but fairly exposed, of course; if ever you are up there with a camera, you should take someone on it, from the head of Deep gh; it looks very well from there. On another day Jeffcoat and I explored the C.B. *[Central Buttress]* and we found a feasible route all the way up, in fact I descended it all on a rope. It is really a most thrilling place. We started down the recess of K.B. *[Keswick Brothers' Climb]* and then worked out to the 'Cannon' (which you will remember). Descending about 80ft from here, we found ourselves by that patch of yellow rock which is so conspicuous a feature of the face; working along to the right I got onto the top of our flake of rock, and managed to traverse this to the end, a thrilling proceeding as the crack at the top of the flake (which is quite tapering and very rough and jagged) is too narrow for the leg. When I got to the end, I descended the overhanging crack, which is very bad for 25 feet. The rope got jammed while I was on this, and I must have spent half an hour struggling with it, so that when at last I managed to move it, I was too tired to go up again, and had to descend to the Oval. At any rate, the C.B. problem is solved as much as it will ever be, I think, and it only remains to make some of the top 25ft of the crack; we ought to do the climb next year some time; it is a most wonderful place, I can assure you, quite the most exciting and sensational I have ever been on, I.C., B.S. *[Botterill's Slab]* etc. included. We did the N.W. *[North-West Climb]* under very greasy conditions, and I found Le Coin and top of Lamb's pretty hard. We also did B.S., which I managed to descend, so that the G.T. *[Girdle Traverse]* will go in the reverse direction.

In essence the two letters, the one to Sansom and the other to Brunskill, are identical. Siegfried went into greater detail when he wrote to Sansom about the problems presented by the jammed rope, confessing that he was 'really in a very awkward position', and he also pointed out that in order to effect the descent, Jeffcoat needed to tie two lengths of rope together, communication between both men being difficult. Sansom had replied from

Brazil and raised a couple of queries, which prompted a second letter from Didsbury, dated September 11th:

> You seem to be staying at Rio longer than you anticipated! To answer your questions about the C.B., I fancy the Flake Crack will turn out quite the severest thing you or I have ever tackled, but I am satisfied as to its feasibility, although none of us actually made the ascent. I expect we will have to wait till next summer for it, unless we have quite exceptional weather at New Year.

It remains to say that the casual reference to Woodhead's Climb was of course to a further new route, now known as Herford's Direct Finish. Fittingly, it was accomplished with Jeffcoat, who had spent anxious hours calmly paying out the rope during the exploratory descent of the Flake, dependable and as solid as the rock itself.

Siegfried's hope that there might be exceptional weather over the New Year failed to materialise. Or rather, it was exceptional, but not in the way he wanted it, for when he reached Wasdale he found the crags plastered in ice and snow, a perilous fairyland. He must have known that Scafell Crag was out of bounds, but by now the rock there had become a passion with him, almost a mission, with its own stirring compulsiveness, and despite what he saw he could not resist the call once again. As the dark year of 1914 dawned, Siegfried, Jeffcoat and Gibson were joined by C.F. Holland, the latter making his first acquaintance with the perpendicular face – and very nearly his last.

Back on what was by now familiar territory, Siegfried led out from the sheltered recess of Moss Ghyll, but it was all vain labour for nobody was going to get very far. The snow-streaked rock was in a desperate state, and the hemp rope, wrinkled and stiffened by jets of ice- water, proved virtually impossible to deal with by hands so cold that they almost ceased to function. A numbed group gathered at the belay toward the end of the ledge where the inevitable decision was taken. From the belay, Siegfried climbed down successfully, despite the snow, although he admitted to being close to the limit, while the others prepared to abseil down in the usual way. Holland, never the most careful of climbers, was then guilty of an act of gross misjudgment. Without waiting to ascertain whether or not the rope was correctly fixed round the belay, he seized it with both hands, and more or less jumped over the ledge. It was a near lethal mistake. His descent, he said 'was a remarkably rapid one', and luckily he came to a stop 25 feet lower, landing on a knob of rock: 'It will always be a proud memory that my ejaculation during this unexpected performance was "God save the

116

King". There are so many things one might have said and regretted it.'
There are indeed! He got away with nothing worse than a bruising.

By the April of 1914, Sansom was back from his expedition to Brazil,
and eager to meet up with the rest of the assault team in his beloved Wasdale.
Jeffcoat was unable to be with them, much to everyone's chagrin, but
Holland and Gibson were there. It turned out a beautiful Easter, and while
patches of snow still lingered on the upper screes, the ransom of winter had
passed, leaving the mountains standing out sharp under a blue of widening
views, and a soft afternoon sunlight wavered across the walls of Scafell. It
was a call to action.

On the 19th, piled up with huge quantities of rope, Siegfried, Sansom,
Holland and Gibson, advanced on their prey: by 11 o'clock they were once
again at the Oval.

The crucial first task was to get to grips with the chockstone in the
Flake Crack. To do this, the party divided into two. Siegfried and Gibson
ascended the Keswick Brothers Climb, from where they traversed out onto
the Central Buttress itself, and positioned themselves in such a way that a
safety rope could be lowered down the crack. Sansom and Holland, meanwhile, had stationed themselves at the Oval: this turned out to be the start
of an historic vigil by Holland. Sansom, having taken off his boots, led up,
but he found the jammed stone, together with the overhanging crack above
it, excessively difficult and he needed a great deal of determined pulling on
the rope from Gibson who was above him. This was a signal for Siegfried
to leave Gibson and get himself back to the Oval, where, taking over from
Sansom, he just managed to heave and edge himself up the chockstone and
crack. This proved that it could be led.

Battle was now well and truly joined. They all re-grouped together at
the Oval, where they rested, preparing for an attack on the chockstone and
crack without the benefit of a rope from above. They had noticed that it
was possible to thread a rope behind the chockstone. Sansom volunteered
to lead back up, fix the thread, and then belay Siegfried as he led the overhanging crack. This is when the old-fashioned hemp rope came into its
own. When the rope became wet, it kinked and stiffened, and using this
fault to advantage, Sansom deliberately soaked two feet of the end of the
rope in wet moss in order to facilitate the threading process. There followed the mother and father of struggles. Six feet below the chockstone,
Sansom found himself precariously placed, and he called out desperately
to Siegfried for a shoulder. Without a moments hesitation, Siegfried moved,
moved fast, and standing on the bulge at the foot of the crack, he steadied
Sansom until he attained a safer position, and was able to use small holds to

reach the chockstone. Siegfried made two valiant assaults on the crack, but the strength in his arms gave out, and a unanimous decision was taken to postpone the attack until the next day, leaving the threaded rope *in situ*. The pipe-smoking Holland, like a latter-day stylite, had endured seven continuous hours belayed at the Oval.

Their luck with the weather held, the 20th dawned fine, and back yet again at the Oval combined tactics were agreed. A second rope was run through the loop. The attack was now poised for one of the most astonishing leads in British rock-climbing history. Sansom, with a vast drop beneath him, just managed to grasp the top of the chockstone while Siegfried used him as an extra foothold. It was determined climbing with a vengeance, one of those ploys that could not last long, and sure enough, Sansom's left hand began to slip from the rock under the strain. Amazingly, Siegfried, at that very moment, unable to get a foot in the position he wanted it, stepped back, and by chance put his foot on the slipping hand and held it in place. Now came the ultimate test, the holdless crack, overhanging by 20 degrees and pushing him physically to the limit: then, with a sudden, swift, inspired cleanness of movement he was up. The Flake Crack had been climbed. He lay exhausted at the top, supported by a jammed knee on the airy rim of the Flake, a solitary figure high above Wasdale, savouring the finest moment of his young life.[4]

Above Flake Crack there remained 200 feet of the Central Buttress still unclimbed and still unexplored. But by then the two-day campaign had left its mark and they had shot their bolt. Confident that the weather was settled, they considered that safety called for a twenty-four truce, so they retired to the valley and delayed their attack on the upper section until the 22nd.

When the troops mustered again, they were without Gibson, who had had to leave for home, and they were joined by Slater. Sansom's account of the climb suddenly introduced the figure of Slater without saying who he was. Edward Vere Slater, to give him his full name, later became known as one of the four 'Eton Masters' who were killed together in a tragic accident in 1933 on Piz Roseg. He was 37 years of age when he became involved with the Central Buttress team, already a master at Eton, but not yet housemaster of The Timbralls. He was an able alpinist, who always preferred to climb with guides, and he had climbed in Norway, but while a safe and average rock-climber, one cannot escape the feeling that on Central Buttress he was out of his depth. Still, obviously, the others thought him good enough to join them, and whatever his ability on rock, he certainly showed pluck.

Siegfried Herford leading the first ascent of the Great Flake

Refreshed from their wise break in climbing, it was a very determined party which approached the upper section, and this time Holland, no longer caged at the Oval, was able to do what he liked best by climbing virgin rock. Sansom takes up the story:

> 50ft above the top of the Great Flake on the Central Buttress is an irregular 'V' shaped grass ledge, from the western end of which springs a wide chimney which is the lower section of the conspicuous Bayonet Shaped Crack running up to the very top of the crags. The upper section of this crack was, we knew, easy. The lower portion looked very unpleasant but we hoped to avoid it by climbing the steep face on the left with Holland and Slater belaying us. We climbed down steep rocks to the 'V' shaped ledge, 100ft below, and from there we were able to look down a remarkably smooth and almost vertical wall to the top of the Great Flake, 50ft lower. The wall was broken at one point by a right angled arête, which in spite of the fact that it overhung slightly, possessed sufficiently good holds to permit of a comfortable descent of 25ft. From its foot, a wonderfully exposed traverse across the almost vertical face on the left enabled us to pass behind a large detached pinnacle and to climb slightly downwards to the shattered ridge against the foot of which the Great Flake abuts.

It was excitingly open climbing, demanding intricate route finding, well suited to prepare Siegfried for the sort of work he would be called upon to tackle in the Alps later in the season. Elated at their discovery, all four climbers came together at the Canon and, belayed from there, Sansom led a traverse up to the 'V' ledge. At that point, Siegfried took over, first trying the Bayonet Shaped Crack, but abandoning it because it looked repulsively hard, from where, seconded by Holland, he started on an exhilaratingly exposed traverse across its foot on to the vertical wall beyond. He moved upwards across the wall for 30ft to a steep slab (now the Herford Slab) which he followed for another 25ft to a good belay at the top of the lower section of the crack. It had been a tremendously committing lead, taking on unknown rock in a very exposed situation, all of it done without so much as the minimum protection of a runner. Here was climbing at its very finest. The others joined him at the belay and climbed easily up the left wall of the upper portion of the Bayonet Shaped Crack, and so to the top of the crag.

What a moment it was to cherish when the dogged Holland could finally say 'the great Central Buttress had really fallen at last'.

Central Buttress, which many had considered inaccessible, firmly established Siegfried's reputation for being right at the forefront of British climbing. There were some in high places, with their old-school suspicion of the young and an ingrained dislike of publicity, who were unhappy at what they felt was a threat to traditional values, but nobody could deny the brilliance of his climbing. It was difficult to keep pace with the sheer intensity of what he did.

An incident occurred right in the middle of the Central Buttress campaign in April 1913. Siegfried, Laycock, and A.R.Thomson, left Manchester on a Saturday morning and drove up to the Lake District in Thomson's car. By early afternoon they were on Iron Crag, Thirlmere, at the head of Shoulthwaite Ghyll, just over three miles south of Keswick. There they climbed the wet and mossy Iron Crag Chimney – 'the rottenest place I have ever been in' – declared Siegfried, then the three of them called on Ashley Abraham at Keswick, who promptly rushed them off to Castle Head in Borrowdale, where they rapidly dissipated whatever energy was still left in them. It had been much the same on another occasion in Langdale. Siegfried and Laycock arrived by chance on May 12th, 1913, at the Old Dungeon Ghyll Hotel only to discover a Wayfarers' Club meet in full swing. Both men were instantly recognised, welcomed, and invited to join in the meet. Siegfried and Laycock's response was to charge up to Pavey Ark, climb the four routes at that time in existence on the crag, dash over to the other side of the valley to scale Bowfell Buttress, and on the following day put up the Wayfarers' Crack on Great End. From the Old Dungeon Ghyll they were able to glance affectionately at one of their new routes, the Middle Fell Buttress, which they had done together eighteen months previously. Middle Fell Buttress is one of those minor gems on which hundreds of nervous beginners have taken their first tentative steps in rock-climbing – and still do so today. If the challenging Central Buttress Climb showed the hard side to Siegfried's character, then Middle Fell Buttress shows him in gentle mood, and he stamped both sides of his nature on the crag-ribbed hills of the Lake District.

CHAPTER TWELVE

THE WATZMANN AND BEYOND

Historians have not written about Siegfried in the context of alpine climbing. It is not difficult to see why. His intense concentration on Scafell, particularly his triumph over the fiercely obdurate Flake Crack, when an inner demon drove him to the limit of his capabilities, marked him out as a quintessentially British-type of rock-climbing ace. Yet there is a case for saying that with Central Buttress the great days on homeland rock had reached their watershed. As far as he was concerned, his gaze had already turned farther afield, new ambitions had begun to stir, the lure of the high places of the Alps, of which he knew little but sensed much. It is doubtful whether he would ever have completely forsaken British rock, but the single-mindedness had come to an end, and it is perhaps significant that the same year in which he spectacularly pulled off the conquest of Central Buttress was later to be crowned by a major success in the Alps.

The Hermann Lietz-Schule schoolboy who negotiated himself to the summit of the Hekla, and then found life a little harder than he had bargained for on the Langjokull icecap, was skilled enough in getting himself safely around British hills, but that was not quite the limit of it. For while by no stretch of the imagination could Siegfried be regarded as experienced on snow-and-ice, the Hekla and the icecap were not the first time he had trodden a glacier.

Siegfried got his first view of alpine peaks in the summer of 1907. The Professor decided that the entire family should add Bavaria to the annual Lake District holiday. The family based themselves at Ramsau, attractively tucked among the Berchtesgaden mountains, and then they all moved on to Caprun. Both Ramsau and Caprun, redolent of the Hapsburgs, still retained their pre-First World War borders, a region in which the traditional felt hat, Tyrolean-style breeches or *lederhosen*, were still very much to be seen.

In Bavaria, as May might have put it, Siegfried was not going to climb in the strict sense of the word, although he did undergo exactly the sort of mountaineering experience designed to excite the imagination of a six-teen-year-old boy. His first alpine peak, tackled under the supervision of a guide, was the Watzmann (8901 feet), hardly a sky-cleaving giant, but still the first one. The Watzmann, with its plentiful and sound rock, had not by then acquired the fame it was to achieve during the interwar years, when the Munich school of climbers carried out their daring artificial climbs and winter ascents. It was on the spectacular East Wall that the driven Hermann Buhl, in 1953, made his solitary winter ascent so as to strengthen and prepare himself for the climbing of Nanga Parbat: he had, he said, to put every fibre of his body and spirit to the test before the time came to sail. Siegfried's outing was straightforward and far less hazardous, but he thoroughly enjoyed it, ending up on the highest of the three summits.

The undoubted *pièce de résistance* of the holiday was the Kitzsteinhorn (10,512 feet), an outlier of the Gross Glockner, which like the main peak stands away from and rises above its neighbours, thereby offering a glorious panoramic view. By the sound of it, all members of the family went part of the way up, certainly as far as the hut, but it is not clear whether the guide then carried on alone with Siegfried; the rather jumbled notes available about the outing imply that that is what happened. Again, we are left to guess about the actual route followed, although here the clear implication points to the Stüdlhütte, in which case Siegfried would have had the easy névé of the Ködnitz for his first glacier. We do know that the climb came to an end up the simple snow arête immediately beneath the summit with the reward of a stunning view. The Kitzsteinhorn had been kinder in that respect than Snowdon. On the way down, by the side of a bluish-white waterfall hidden in a small ravine, Siegfried stumbled across an edelweiss.

The somewhat sparse information available to us about the Bavarian holiday does not permit us to go beyond the Watzmann and the Kitzsteinhorn. But there is an interesting footnote. All members of the family were fluent German speakers and could converse with the guide on equal terms. It is pure speculation, granted, but not beyond bounds to imagine Siegfried pressing the guide about the technicalities of snow work in his own language. This is even more likely when we learn that the two of them struck up a friendship and corresponded until the outbreak of war.

Five years were to elapse before Siegfried again climbed on foreign soil. This time it was in the Dolomites, in the July of 1912, with George Sansom as his partner.

Siegfried wrote an account of the trip for the 1913 *Fell and Rock Climbing Club Journal*, entitled 'Two Famous Dolomite Climbs', describing the Winkler and Fünffingerspitze respectively. He opened his article in an uncharacteristically parochial mood:

> Nevertheless, the English-bred climber will find a visit well worthwhile, if only for the grandeur of the scenery, and for the opportunity of observing the methods of the German school of cragsmen. He will learn the art of moving quickly and safely on easy rock of

doubtful quality, of which there is an excessive amount on most peaks. If he is climbing guideless, he will have excellent practice in route finding and will on many occasions have to invent a way of his own. If, on the other hand, he is attached to a guide, he may have the pleasure of seeing him grow intensely excited over a ten-foot pitch about as hard as Kern Knotts Chimney, and of finding himself hailed as the greatest climber of the day, should he fail to make a hopeless bungle of it.

Probably, he was writing with tongue in cheek, for it is difficult to believe he meant what he said about the quality of Dolomitic rock, and it was hardly like him to show how English he was by poking fun at the Germans.

Despite the somewhat dismissive remarks, we learn that both men were impressed by the Vajolet Towers, and thoroughly enjoyed climbing the Winkler. It was their sort of climb. The Winkler, a famous solo ascent by the seventeen-year-old Munich student Georg Winkler, epitomised their own approach to a large extent. Georg Winkler himself was certainly a less prudent operator than either Siegfried or Sansom, and would pay the ultimate price for his gifted recklessness [1], but he showed the same flair for a line, and on rock shared the same technical grasp and grit. The adopted route started by taking the narrow chimney separating the Winkler itself from the Stabeler. During the ascent an incident occurred which showed how implicitly the two men had come to trust each other. At one point they found themselves off course, blocked by a succession of terraces over one of those enormous Dolomitic drops of a thousand feet or more (Siegfried would later compare the exposure on Central Buttress to the Dolomites); then, having solved the problem, Siegfried led to within 20 feet of the summit, where he discovered that the rope behind him had run out. He was forced to remain where he was, unbelayed on a small hold, until Sansom moved up behind him unprotected. It was an airy manoeuvre, with no room for any miscalculation, an act of trust they almost took for granted.

Ten days later they turned their attention to the Fünffingerspitze. What climbs they did during the interval between the two peaks is a blank, one of the penalties for not being able to locate Siegfried's climbing log, but it is certain they were far from inactive. Siegfried sent May a postcard telling her they were about to tackle the Fünffingerspitze, which he told his sister was 'really the last word in climbing', and he assured her they were both feeling very fit and ready for the climb.

Perhaps the awesome and exaggerated reputation the Fünffingerspitze enjoyed at the time, owed something to the writing of Ludwig Norman-Neruda. Swedish by birth, a Londoner by adoption, Norman-Neruda had a lifetime's love affair with the Fünffingerspitze, climbing it six times with his great guide Christian Klucker, and meeting his untimely death on it due to a fall. He pointed out that the 'five' ought not to be taken too literally, for while the peak did have a general resemblance to a hand, 'you must not be too accurate in counting the fingers'.

Siegfried and Sansom had set their sights on climbing the Fünffingerspitze by the Schmitt Kamin, a route that at the time had a reputation for being difficult and tricky, and as a preliminary reconnaissance they first went up to the summit by using the ordinary Daumenscharte route. They were fit, and had moved very fast, so by the afternoon they were ready for the real thing and found themselves at the top of the initial series of slabs that lead to the foot of the Kamin.

Both men were unimpressed by the first section of the Kamin itself, finding it monotonously easy, Siegfried saying that the rotten rock reminded him of mouldy biscuits. At the Kirchl, an 80-feet cave pitch, Sansom led, finding the final pull out over the chockstone robbed of its terrors by a large foothold on one wall. This was followed by a short scree promenade leading to an overhanging chimney, wide to start with, but narrowing as it got higher. Sansom wriggled himself into position, using a right-hand wall notable for its absence of holds, and with a heave over a capstone he was up. From there they lost the line of the route. Because of this, they were compelled to make a sensational stride on to an opposite wall, crawl gingerly along a ledge made up of rotten rock, and before any harm was done, they realised their mistake and made a tactical retreat. Once back at the top of the chimney they had forsaken, Siegfried took over the lead, reaching a fine 100-feet chimney that he compared to Collier's Chimney in Moss Ghyll. Half way up the chimney, he found an excellent stance and belay, which enabled Sansom to follow through up a steep projecting wall. That constituted the last serious pitch of the climb, the angle eased off, and they reached the summit for the second time that day by moving quickly up some slabs on the right. They were content to mooch slowly down by the ordinary route and regain the hut.

The trip to the Dolomites had been a relaxed holiday, to be enjoyed with Sansom, and the description of the Winkler and Schmitt Kamin made no exaggerated claim. A number of standard routes had been tackled unguided with the level of competency one might expect of both men. When, in 1914, Siegfried again found himself in the Alps, the position was very different. The scene was set for a vital move forward. The meeting with Winthrop Young on the chill eyrie of Tryfan signalled the start of a significant change of direction.

From the moment Siegfried found himself embroiled in the Pen-y-Pass scene, the Alps began to beckon. His gaze turned to a different type of mountain world beyond the dark sepulchre of the Oval sunk into the indomitable Scafell granite. At Pen-y-Pass he encountered the *crème de la crème* of the Alpine Club, a strata of the hierarchy, both in social and climbing terms, new to him, for whom Central Buttress was not their type of climbing, and who assessed reputations by what had been achieved in the Alps, or even farther afield. Winthrop Young, with perfect timing, waited for the consummation of Central Buttress and then pounced, whisking off to the Oberland the aloof Sun-god he deemed the future of mountaineering. There was not the slightest hint of condescension about it. His plans for the 1914 season demanded the inclusion of a rock-climber in the party and he determined on the best man available. Siegfried by then was ready and willing.

In the July, Siegfried found himself introduced to one of the most outstanding partnerships between amateur and professional in the whole history of alpine climbing, that between Winthrop Young and Joseph Knubel. The *litterateur* and the stonemason carried out a collection of dazzling expeditions, some of the finest seen prior to the First World War, and in several instances not repeated until after the Second World War. A special bond existed between the two climbers, with only the chosen few allowed to intrude upon it, which in itself is a measure of how far Siegfried had come. Winthrop Young's great organisational flair came into play. He realised that Knubel and himself were both considerably senior in age, and to avoid the risk of leaving Siegfried isolated, he accepted Knubel's recommendation that a young guide by the name of Hans Brantschen should be included in the party. Straight-backed, strong, tough, and very fast, Brantschen was a young man of few words, almost as clam-like as Siegfried. It is quite obvious that by bringing the two younger climbers together, Winthrop Young had a long-term purpose in mind: he hoped they would take to each other and forge their own partnership as the years went by. Destiny was not to allow that hope to come to fruition. Brantschen went on to carve out for himself a distinguished career as a guide, taking part in a series of notable ascents, and we are left with one of the great might-have-beens in alpine history. The truth of this is underlined by the way the two of them hit if off immediately and climbed brilliantly together.[2]

Siegfried's departure for the Alps was delayed by obligations at the Royal Aircraft Factory, where he was caught up in a research project. This enabled Young, Knubel and Brantschen to get in a training climb before he could join them. They selected the Bietschhorn, a 'bedraggled' peak according to Young, his three previous attempts on it having been defeated by bad weather. The party succeeded this time, but again the weather was bad, forcing them to descend in a sizzling electric storm. Their climb proved an ominous portent, for the rest of the season would be spent dodging storms, with a great deal of waiting around for the peaks to clear.

Winthrop Young's chief objective was the unclimbed Rote Zähne (West Ridge) of the Gspaltenhorn. This gaunt ridge, a series of formidable towers or teeth, had already repulsed a number of strong parties. It was chiefly a rock route, with snow mixed in, and Siegfried had been recruited to play to his strengths.

Winthrop Young wrote two accounts of his climbs during the 1914 season. One can be found in his autobiographical, *On High Hills*, one of the best of his books.[3] In the *Alpine Journal* he elaborated more specifically on the technicalities of the Rote Zähne itself, although he covered more ground than that.[4] The problem we have is that the two versions do not always tally with each other. Quite early on we run into difficulty about dates. We know for certain that the onset of bad weather on the Bietschhorn was a signal for Winthrop Young and the two guides to move over to the Gamchi hut, so as to be well placed for an immediate attack on the Gspaltenhorn ridge. From the Gamchi, Winthrop Young went down to Gries Alp, there to greet Siegfried on his arrival, and they both walked back up to the hut under an overcast sky. The issue is, when did this take place, July 6th or July 7th? Behind the question lies the issue of whether or not Siegfried took part in a first ascent. In the book version of events, Winthrop Young said that on July 6th, anxious to get a good view of the Rote Zähne, he, Knubel and Brantschen went to the summit of the Gspaltenhorn by the ordinary route, in other words, by way of the Gamchi-Lücke, but they were discouraged to find their ridge plastered in snow and out of condition. They had moved fast – Brantschen always did – taking a mere three hours, so, on descending back to the Büttlasson Lücke, they called a halt. Then they had something to eat, organised their ropes, and as time was very much in their favour, they made the first ascent of the Büttlasson South Ridge. There is no mention of Siegfried having been with them. This is because, according to the book, it was the next day, the 7th, that Winthrop Young went down to Gries Alp to meet him. In the *Alpine Journal*, however, the dates are reversed and Siegfried is credited with the Büttlasson climb which is stated to have taken place on the 7th, and it is this version which has found its way into the guide book. The best we can do is to look at the overall chronology, and this tends to suggest that it is the *Alpine Journal* version that is the more accurate of the two.

Whatever the truth about the date, there was no doubt about the awful weather, the distant boom of avalanches between the irksome sound of hail rumbling on the roof, the Rote Zähne being firmly out of bounds. Knubel was gloomy about their chances: 'We have never yet been turned back', he complained, 'except by storm, *but*' – and it was an emphatic 'but'! A smouldering frustration left the two younger men roving around inside the hut like caged lions. However, release would soon be on the way. Not all that far from the Gamchi hut, facing it lower down the valley, stood both the Wilde Frau and the neighbouring Morgenhorn. At the time, in 1914, neither peak had yet been ascended from the Gamchi glacier side. Here, if only the weather relented somewhat, might prove an interesting alternative to the main objective of the Gspaltenhorn ridge. The opportunity came on July 9th, which dawned fine, or almost fine, certainly without snow falling, and the Wilde Frau stood out clear. It was only a slight chance, the hint of a possibility, but when it came to alpine climbing that is all Winthrop Young and Knubel ever needed: they shared a tested instinct and knew exactly the right moment to make a move. Siegfried was in for an object lesson on gathering rosebuds while you may.

The party swiftly left the hut and set out for the unclimbed north-east ridge of the Wilde Frau. The four of them trudged up to the high, snow plateau now glinting on the northern side of the Blümlisalp massif, then struck up the black-looking ridge that sticks out from the summit of the peak. The ridge ought to have presented few obstacles to such a talented party, but they were hardly climbing under optimum conditions, and Winthrop Young admitted that as they straddled the huge precipice which spills menacingly to the south, he felt that they were up against as much as they could handle. Slowly, they edged up the broken surface of the ridge, piled with snow, and, having lost sight of each other in the intermittent squalls of powdery drift, were mightily relieved to reach the summit. They made quick progress down to the shelter of the Blümlisalp hut, which, by good fortune, had only recently been constructed. For Siegfried, the climb had offered a new level of snow work, and for it he could not have been in better company. Lietz's Guardian had been under the tutelage of General Young, and Sergeant Major Knubel, and nothing silly was going to happen as it had done on the Langjokull.

The break in the bad weather was to continue, with one of those sharply magical alpine nights, with stars blinking on the snow covering the roof of the hut. When sunrise came, mists floated over the Oeschinsee below, flecked by green and blue and patches of moving roseate, a panorama of crag and snow coming alive again across the vista of the Gemmi. There was no question of going for the coveted Rote Zähne, which needed a good three days of sun for it to get into condition, so the party wisely decided to turn necessity into pleasure and started out on a long high-level walk.

The route from the Gamchi Lücke to Bel Alp abounded with views of glacial scenery, taking in the Petersgrat, the Lötschental, and the Beich pass – if not the Oberland at its most sublime, then certainly commanding a magnificent prospect. All of it was entirely new ground for Siegfried. Winthrop Young set out on the stunning trek with a troubled mind, wondering how Siegfried would react. His concern was that Siegfried might feel disappointed, justifiably looking for chosen peaks, big climbs, regarding an alpine walk as second best. But not a bit of it. Winthrop Young's concern was understandable, yet unfounded, and he began to glimpse a fresh insight into his two silent protégés, Siegfried and Brantschen, as they strung along rhythmically side by side. He started to appreciate more about Siegfried's response to the mountain world, a response founded in boyhood, on his solitary wanders around the Lake District hills. Winthrop Young wrote:

> He enjoyed it, if anything, even more than I. Peaks could wait.
> This is what he came to the Alps for – what only the Alps could give.

He noticed how, when they reached the crest of the steep wall of the Beich Pass, Siegfried showed the same sureness of foot and eye on snow, the same perfect balance, he had made pre-eminent on British rock. Siegfried never ecstasised enchantment; 'the blue remembered hills' were not his style, and while on one rare occasion, on Helvellyn with his mother, he gave vent to his feelings, his usual custom was to absorb himself in Oriental silence. In Brantschen he had found a fellow traveller in that respect.

By July 14th, conditions had improved beyond all recognition, and at last, the Rote Zähne was ready for them, and they for it.

Encouragingly, the night was a really cold one, and by 3.45 in the morning the party had already scampered across the glacier. They were quickly at grips with a great open snow couloir, which needed as much care as it did skill, and after tackling a series of easy slabs, they stood on the skyline of the main ridge. They had joined the ridge some way below a first, conspicuous rock step, not far from a sensational looking needle. Siegfried and Brantschen, who by now were climbing easily together, smiled at each other in anticipation. They were, in fact, at the first Red Tooth, and they were taken by surprise to discover that in an odd fashion the Tooth projected out of the North Face, the true crest of the ridge passing behind it. The hard struggle they fully expected to have failed to materialise and in an unexpectedly short time they found themselves standing on top of the Tooth.

The real difficulties of the climb loomed starkly ahead of them. The first of many abseils had now to be executed. To do this, they clambered down over the wall-corner of a smooth grey slab for some 20 feet, and then utilised a crazy looking gargoyle for hitching the rope. The initial drop took them down 60 feet, to a cramped but firm stance, followed by a second drop of 80 feet, which allowed them to reach a V-shaped gash that separated the first Tooth from the second. Flake Crack, on Central Buttress, had offered a hard initiation into the mysteries of rope mechanics, and the others were quick to spot how businesslike Siegfried was in handling them. They were now committed, stuck in the V-gap, with the only exit a direct assault on the colossal wall which blocked their progress. Brantschen took the lead, climbing into the unknown with nerve, and, taking what advantage he could of a number of tiny fissures, he found himself standing on a dangerously precipitous corner, from where he elbow-wriggled up an overhang, then finished by taking on a series of highly exposed and broken pitches up the final steep wall. Thanks to this fine piece of climbing, all four crowded together on the top of the second Tooth, reaching it by 10.45.

The ideal conditions were too good to last, and while at that point of the climb the air began to chill, all thought of retreat was unthinkable; they were far too much into the climb for that. What lay ahead of them, however, was hardly encouraging. A huge gulf followed the formidable tusk on which they stood. Knubel led down by using the northern edge of the second Tooth, and after reaching the base of the gash, moving to and fro as he searched for possibilities, he traversed delicately over a section of broken rock covered by ice so as to reach a fantastic flying buttress, beneath which lay an appalling sweep of slabs extending the entire length of the ridge down to the glacier. A series of elaborate manoeuvres forced a way to a tottering rock-comb, from where a further 60 foot abseil was fixed, leading down to an unlikely col. They were then right up against the crest of the third Red Tooth. From behind, the Tooth was joined to the summit mass, which was a relief to know, but to reach it they had first to turn north by way of an airy traverse. This involved moving cautiously down a steep couloir, in which the snow adhered at an angle of 60 degrees, followed by 200 feet of balancing across icy slabs, after which came a narrow chimney caked with ice. But they could see their objective. Once out of the chimney, and across a few more slabs, they emerged on to an arête directly in line with the third Tooth now well below them. At 1.45 the victorious team celebrated on the summit of the Gspaltenhorn, a ten-hour climb from the hut. It took them a mere 62 minutes to get back there, and with conditions once more in their favour, they spent the rest of the day basking in the sun.

Top: On the first tower of the Rote Zähne, Gspaltenhorn. Knubel left, Brantschen, Herford right. Foot: The Rote Zähne from the first tower

It is difficult to imagine Siegfried having a more technically demanding, yet at the same time more satisfying, third season in the Alps. The weather had not been kind, but time and opportunity had been well used, and a number of good climbs were on record. The Rote Zähne in particular had been a testing undertaking. Paul Montandon, who made the third ascent of the route in 1919, was duly impressed by it:

> We again and again wondered at the boldness of thought which made him (i.e. Winthrop Young) conceive and undertake this tour – and many others of similar daring – and the determination and strong confidence which induced his party everywhere to draw down their rope after having abseiled. [5]

Montandon made a strong point. During the climb the risk entailed in pulling down the abseil rope after them had more than once been the subject of anxious discussion. In the gap after they had roped down the first Tooth, Siegfried, in a perfectly calm voice, volunteered to climb back up the smooth slab with his boots off had the party found themselves unable to move forward. It was not the sort of thing one was expected to do on such a climb. What saw them through was confidence in themselves.

Having done what they set out to do, the party moved over to Zermatt, once again new ground for Siegfried.

The weather at Zermatt proved no more settled than it had been in the Oberland. They were rather depressed when all the reports confirmed that none of the big peaks were 'going'. This was the first time Siegfried had set eyes on the Matterhorn, the great dramatic pyramid, with its geometric lines sweeping upwards to the sky, and it looked as if the opportunity to climb it would pass him by. But what was new to Siegfried was an old friend to Winthrop Young; he knew exactly how to read the mountain. Sure enough, from his hotel window, he spotted the key sign; the Zmutt ridge was the only one in the valley that remained black due to the violent winds which had swept the snow off it. Again, it was only half a chance; but again that was all he needed. In the dash up to the Schönbiel hut, Winthrop Young and Knubel found it impossible to keep pace with their two younger companions, and they fell hopelessly behind. There is some confusion about whether or not the party roped up for the Zmutt. Winthrop Young's private *Journal* said not:

> Up the snow-covered crags of the ridge to the summit we all went separately for the greater speed; and still unroped we raced down the eastern shoulder to Zermatt, beating the return rush of the snow-blizzard up the valley by a few minutes. [6]

Herford, front, Brantschen and Knubel, rear, on the Zmutt Arête   Photo: G W Young

That is not what he wrote in the 1916 *Alpine Journal*, where we are told they did rope, the older men on one and the younger sharing the other. Either way, it was a fast climb, the windswept ridge falling to them romantically and magnificently.

The Zmutt Ridge effectively ended the season. Siegfried and Winthrop Young elected to spend the final day of the holiday bathing from a small boat on Lac Léman. They talked about this and that, talked endlessly about mountains, little realising that all they might have cherished and hoped for in the world of mountaineering, and open winds, had already come to an end. A glint of light reflected from the uneasy shadows in the water, while behind the cloud gathering over the Jura to the north, all the livid steeds of the Apocalypse were gathering force, making ready to ravish and consume Siegfried and so many of his generation. Their moment together on the lake marked more than the end of a holiday.

WAR

1914 – 1916

I've shared the friendship of these men
Upon great crags, and in the glen.
In snow and ice, on rocky bands,
And scaling cliffs from shadow'd sands.

Lofoten, Dieppe, St Nazaire!
Names that will stand for courage rare.
Deeds that will shine, undimm'd by Age
In England's book, an honoured Page.

T'is true that on the Hills I find
That all men see each other's mind.
In depth not known upon the Plains
Veneer is stripped, and what remains?

I find born cragsmen, with steady nerve,
But more, I see I humbly serve
Brave hearts, with noble virtues graced
By God, who made their stalwart Race.

Commando   A.W. Bridge
(Written during the Second World War)

CHAPTER THIRTEEN

THE GOD OF MARS

In the July of 1914, at almost the precise moment that Siegfried arrived at Gries Alp to be greeted by Winthrop Young at the start of their stormy alpine season, vast crowds had packed Portsmouth shore to witness the thrilling spectacle of a 45-mile long line of warships strung out beyond Spithead, the most formidable concentration of sea-power the world had ever seen, a symbol of Britain's naval supremacy. Few among the cheering spectators realised that within only a few weeks of the display, all the ships, resplendent in their colourful flags, would put to sea in earnest. Britain had found itself embroiled in the most terrifying war of all time. 'The lamps are going out all over Europe', declared Lord Grey, on August 3rd, the day Britain's ultimatum to Germany expired, 'and we shall not see them lit again in our lifetime'. Names like Jutland and Passchendale and the Somme would be ingrained in every household at Portsmouth.

Instant patriotic hullabaloo followed the declaration of war. It seemed as if every town in the land was anxious to raise at least one battalion. 'It will all be over by Christmas', was the popular refrain, and streams of young men, many of them unemployed, poured into the Town Halls to enlist, cheerfully oblivious of what they were letting themselves in for. They were to find that whatever hope or aspirations they held were to be crushed in a harrowing bloodbath on an immense scale. The grizzly estimate is that over a four-year period 5,600 servicemen per day died on the battlefield. For them the kind old sun did not know. Within two years, particularly after the terrible casualties of the Somme, those who managed to survive increasingly found themselves belonging to a demoralised generation.

Didsbury found itself caught up in the turmoil. The excited activity, the frenzied mood, the emotional fervour, all seemed so far distant from the golden days of Aberystwyth. When Siegfried and May planned and peopled their imaginary world on planet Mars, and crowned themselves kings, it was inconceivable that their two closely allied countries could ever go to war against each other. But Mars was the Roman god of war; and Mars was on the march. The stark fact was that their two imaginary countries were replicated by two real countries, England and Germany, both of them lands with a family ancestry. The lamps, if anywhere, had indeed gone out on planet Mars.

*Marie Herford (seated),
May and Siegfried at
5 Parkfield Rd, Didsbury
in 1915*

A group of Royal Fusiliers: Siegfried on the left

No member of Siegfried's household bore a heavier burden than his mother. The onset of war hurled her into nothing less than a family tragedy and the implications of it sent shudders down to the very heart. Her husband was an Englishman, her daughter and son were English, but she was German, her much-loved parents who still lived in Bremen were German, her grandparents were German. What could she, or any person, make of such a conflict of loyalties? It was as if each country had issued a licence for her kith-and-kin to kill each other. She had to carry a grief without any resolution which could make much sense. Her advice to her son, therefore, was all the more astonishing: 'It is your country', she told him laconically, 'and you must fight for it.'

There seemed to be little point in Siegfried keeping on with his aeronautical work at Farnborough. The Government had made their policy quite clear. The Government believed that Britain's strength lay where it always had done in the past, on the sea and not in the air, and to that end they had authorised a massive ship-building programme. By then, in any event, he had completed his own research which would gain him an M.Sc.. He had then to brace himself to face the outbreak of hostilities and his mother's injunction: he did so by applying for a commission as an army officer.

Siegfried never harboured any doubt in his own mind that his commission would come through, but he fully recognised that the War Office was inundated with applications, each one having to be processed separately, and that inevitably a delay would occur before he heard anything. Rather than wait around, aimlessly kicking his heels before he was notified, he took up a proposal made by Winthrop Young. Winthrop Young, somewhat unexpectedly it must be said, had landed the job of war correspondent for the *Daily News*, and the suggestion was for Siegfried to join him in France as his Secretary-Assistant on the newspaper. Neither of them could have imagined, when they said goodbye in the Oberland, that they would be thrown together again so unexpectedly.

Winthrop Young realised from the start that getting dispatches back to London was not going to be straightforward, and he was anxious to enrol Siegfried, whom he knew to be vigorous and determined, as someone he could rely on. Accordingly, on September 2nd, Siegfried was issued with a special passport (No.102931) on which he was designated as 'Mr Siegfried Wedgwood Herford; British subject travelling in France'. The accreditation of him as a 'British subject' turned out to be a godsend. On both sides of the channel the atmosphere was panicky, and officialdom was highly suspicious of a young man with a German name who appeared to be constantly getting on and off boats or trains. More than once, especially in

France, he had to stand his ground. Being Secretary-Assistant to Winthrop Young, however, did not last long. His energetic temperament did not take kindly to the role of carrier-pigeon and he quickly became frustrated. He was only doing the job because he was waiting for his commission to come through, but this seemed to be taking longer than he expected, and he had started to feel that he wanted to be closer to the real action. Winthrop Young, of course, was disappointed when he left, although he fully understood how he felt, for Young was feeling rather the same way himself.

Siegfried's next move might very well have been influenced by May. His sister had volunteered as a nurse with the Red Cross, and it was in that direction that he now turned, offering to act temporarily as ambulance chauffeur until the War Office notified him.

Once again he had to go through the routine of filling in piles of forms. By November 8th the formalities were complete when he was issued with Army Form C.337: 'British Empire. Army Certificate of Identity for Civilians Wearing the Red Cross Brassard. Certificate No.1390'. As protected personnel, he was required to wear an armlet - or brassard - with a red cross on a white background, to be fixed to the left arm. Regulations governing that sort of thing were specific: 'The Brassard should be STITCHED to the left sleeve above the elbow'. The 'stitched' was written in capital letters so as to avoid any misunderstanding by a mere civilian. He was also placed under the orders of the Commander-in-Chief.

It is difficult to know how Siegfried visualised an ambulance driver's life on the battlefield. The work was arduous, with long hours, drivers often finding themselves in the line of fire. They were expected to keep calm, and on top of the job, in a frenzied atmosphere; saving lives or carting the dead. He drove a 14 h.p. Hurlu, a stout vehicle, capable of tackling the worst roads imaginable or negotiating around shell-torn villages potted with holes. (*Motor Magazine*, March 23rd, 1915, published a picture showing Siegfried standing by a Hurlu ambulance.) The drill was for the wounded to make their first journey by stretcher bearers, who took them to a dressing station out of the range of artillery fire, and from there they would be moved back down to a clearing hospital. In reality a dressing station could well be within the range of fire, and on many an occasion a driver would have to jump from his vehicle into a trench, lifting a wounded soldier out by whatever means were to hand. It was a rough and dangerous life.

Siegfried wrote two accounts of his work with the Red Cross, both published in *The Manchester Guardian*, the first dated January 2nd, 1915:

WAR SIDELIGHTS

THE HAZARDOUS WORK OF THE
MOTOR AMBULANCE

From a letter received on New Year's
Eve from a Manchester ambulance motorist
at the front.
North of France.

We have been having a busy time lately. On Sunday we had orders
to go immediately to Château ... about seven miles from here ... to clear a
large number of wounded out, as the place was being shelled. We dashed
off as hard as we could. The shelling turned out not to be serious, just an
occasional shrapnel. The only warning you get is the singing of the shell,
and a second or two later a terrific clap, quite different – much sharper –
from the thud made by the firing of the gun itself. No-one appeared to have
been hurt, though one or two bits of shrapnel came down close by on the
road. Meanwhile the wounded had to be got out, and as there were several
hundred of them, and only a few cars, this was a matter of some time.

Something in the nature of panic seems to have taken place among
them, as on the road away from the front were large numbers limping, and
in some cases crawling along on hands and knees. In more than one instance I saw their wounds had started bleeding again, and they had collapsed on the roadside. Some of the cars had quite a time picking up these
people and conveying them to the field hospital. We were busy with this
work till about ten at night, when our car, with two others, had orders to go
on to the aid-post by the trenches and evacuate them. The way was along a
narrow road by the side of the ... Canal, and the front car succeeded in
falling partially into a ditch by the side of the road. This was no joke, for,
try as we could, we were unable to shift it. It was a good job it was dark, as
the spot was in view of the German trenches, and had in fact been swept by
machine guns that day. It was therefore imperative to get the car out before
dawn, and two horses were requisitioned for the job.

In the meanwhile our car ran backwards along the canal (a tricky
business with the water one side and a ditch on the other) on the main road,
about a mile. In trying to get past us an ambulance waggon with two mules
managed to fall into the canal, and we had a nice business getting them out
– i.e. the mules only; the waggon we, personally, left to its fate. We eventually went round to the aid-post by a decent road, doing the usual crawl in

the dark for the last mile or so. Things were pretty lively just then, as an attack (by the British) was going on just outside the village we were in. Leaving the cars under the shelter of a large brewery, we hurried across the canal bridge to the house where the wounded were lying. By the dim candle light we could see that the floor was pretty well covered with them. There were six Germans among them. One was lying in the corner mortally wounded. The others were carried away to the cars on stretchers, saying farewell to their comrade, Adolf (quite a boy) as they passed.

Bullets were pretty plentiful as we passed along the canal and over the bridge, and it was lucky that no-one was hit. We had two Germans in our car. One was pretty bad, shot through the lungs. They were very thankful when we took them off at the hospital. By this time it was getting on for dawn, and we had an ordinary day's work to get through. We slept well that night, but were unfortunately turned out at 3 a.m. for more work, which kept us going most of the day. The next night's rest was also broken from 12 to 3 a.m. So we were feeling rather weary on Wednesday.

[the blanks above are due to wartime editing]

Knowing what we now do about what happens to information during a war – the first casualty of war is truth – it is extraordinary that *The Manchester Guardian* felt able or willing to publish Siegfried's letter. What stands out is not so much the half-expected insouciance – bullets were pretty plentiful – but the humanity of the piece, the sense of chivalry. The picture of the German soldiers filing out in the dim candlelight saying their farewells to the mortally wounded boy Adolf has a pathos worthy of Erich Maria Remarque's *All Quiet on the Western Front*. The wounded Tommies Siegfried and his crew plucked from out of the firing line would have felt little or no animosity towards the German casualties sharing the ambulance with them. This was in marked contrast to the angry mood back at home. In Britain itself the Government propaganda machine had successfully whipped up intense anti-German feeling and a xenophobia against all things German. Not only were anti-German slogans to be seen daubed on the walls, but those with even the slightest association with Germany, such as a German name, ran the risk of being physically assaulted in the street. Earl Mountbatten's father, a Battenberg, found himself mercilessly mocked for his German origin and was hounded from high office. It was an hostile atmosphere Marie Herford must have found virtually intolerable. The mood certainly destroyed the Manchester German community which had been the backbone of Lady Barn House School. In that context it must have taken *The Manchester Guardian* some courage to publish Siegfried's second letter, in which he made the point, no doubt to the astonishment of many of his readers:

> With regard to the Germans, the opinion seems to be general that as far as the British are concerned – i.e. outside of Belgium – the Germans have behaved much better than is made out, and the British officer has certainly great admiration for the German soldier.

This is a point repeated in Lyn Macdonald's brilliant book, *Somme*, where she points out that there was plenty of anti-German ribaldry to be found in the dugouts, but alongside it went a mild tolerance, the Germans being referred to familiarly as Fritz.[1] The Tommies in Siegfried's ambulance understood what those at home did not, that trench warfare is a dirty business, dirty for men on both sides of the wire, and but for the grace of God the dying Adolf might well have been one of themselves.

Chauffeuring for the Red Cross was essential war work, and well worth doing, but it was not what Siegfried wanted; or rather, it was not what he thought he wanted at the time. What he wanted was for the War Office to make a move about his application for a commission.

The War Office made no such move. From their point of view, the application presented a clear risk, and swamped with work as they were, they were in no mood to take a risk. The minuses against the application added up. The applicant had a German mother; he himself carried a German name; and not only had he been partially educated at a German school, more fundamentally, he had undergone a German military training at a cadet officer level. Nor did the case against him stop there. England in 1914 was still very much two nations, as sharply divided as it ever had been in Victorian times, and his northern background proved an obvious deterrent. The War Office expected aspirants for a commission to be 'gentlemen', but, from where they sat, they considered anywhere in the north to be 'almost wholly without a professional stratum and so without an officer class'. [2] On top of this blinkered attitude, Siegfried had blotted his copy book by writing his letters to *The Manchester Guardian*. The two letters, it is true, had been published anonymously, but with spy mania as rampant as it was, it would not have taken a War Office official ten minutes to discover the author's true identity. They would certainly have been anxious to know who the writer was. Not only did a young man with German links make favourable comments about the Germans, he added for good measure that he witnessed panic among the allied ranks, an almost treasonable admission in those fraught days. Those running the Government propaganda machine would have been horrified to read the description of the crawling wounded collapsed and bleeding by the road-side. That was the last thing they wanted people to know about. Civilian support for a war tends to be undermined as the cost in casualties builds up. Looked at from an official point of view, Siegfried's application for a commission had little to commend it, and quite clearly at some point along the line a decision had been made to play safe.

Both John Laycock and C.E. Montague, who saw Siegfried as a man of outstanding leadership qualities, are on record as saying how incredulous they felt that the War Office should refuse him a commission. But there is no evidence among family papers which points to a refusal. The people in charge at the War Office may have been class ridden, blinkered and arrogant, but they were better trained than that. They adopted the time-honoured method of conveying their intentions by saying absolutely nothing, by ignoring Siegfried completely, suspecting that if the silence went on long enough the message would finally get home. In this assumption they were right. We know from Siegfried's childhood days that this usually rational, calmly deliberate man, capable of standing for twenty minutes on the same hold before prudently making the next move up a rock face, nevertheless had the ability to exhibit a fiery impulsiveness. By February, 1915, after working four months with the Red Cross, frustrated, angry, not used to being ignored by anybody, his patience finally snapped. Emotions of that sort hardly provide a springboard for wise decision making, and in what was clearly a crucially precipitate action, he resigned from the Red Cross and enlisted as a ranker in the 2nd Sportman's Battalion, later the 24th Royal Fusiliers, an overspill of the 23rd Battalion. When the Professor posthumously commented on his enlistment he said his son had taken 'the one way open to him'. But that was far from the case. Other quite justifiable options were open to him. One option was for him to have stayed with the Red Cross. Another might have been to use his engineering knowledge at the Royal Aircraft Factory, for he was exactly the sort of man able to persuade the authorities that aircraft had a part to play in the war, and if later an urge to do his share of the fighting still rankled, he could have copied what his climbing partner George Sansom did and joined the Royal Flying Corps. His decision to enlist as a private was not the one way open to him and it comes over more as an angry reaction to the War Office's calculated snub.

Siegfried's life then took on an entirely different complexion and it would never be the same again. Between the February of 1915, when his enlistment in the Royal Fusiliers took place, and the November when his embarkation to the front became due, he looked the same as all the other thousands of volunteers who buckled down to learning the unfamiliar trade of soldiering. A sort of inexorable inevitability takes hold of a trainee soldier's life in wartime, being shuttled from one training camp to another, each one marking a stage to a predestined embarkation. Siegfried, who since boyhood had struggled to control and direct his mind and body – a mastery eventually forged on the anvil of rock – had seemingly surrendered himself to an impersonal logic leading to a conclusion over which he had no control. But that was only how it seemed on the surface. Siegfried was too complicated a man, too much an enigma and with too strong a character for the position he was in to be tolerated for too long. Inwardly nothing was placid or orderly and the khaki drill of external circumstances covered up the true state of affairs. It was not so much the urge to take control again that had surfaced, but more importantly he had come to realise what he had left out of account when he made his impulsive decision to enlist: he had come to see the importance of the life-saving work of the Red Cross, to acknowledge the impact the period of chauffeuring had had on him, and that caring for the wounded carried with it its own vindication and confirmation of manhood. He would apply himself at training camp with characteristic thoroughness, but inwardly he was again at odds with himself and was beginning to lay a plan for a way forward, a plan designed to unlock the tortuous situation he found himself in – to a large extent of his own making.

The exigencies of total war render personal decision making either very simple or infinitely complex. Pressures can build up on all sides, some ethical and based on conviction, others more personal, like the expectations of family or peers, and the young especially have to take regard of the imperatives of valour, often magnificently misplaced and mistaken, but always burning and urgent. For those who are caring and thoughtful, like Siegfried, war acts as a bloody catalyst for change and will leave no stone of the soul unturned; thoughts and feelings and relationships are pitchforked cruelly into a nightmare. Those whose loyalties are simple face no such dilemmas. Siegfried began simply and he was clear about where his duty lay; 'It is your country and you must fight for it' . He was never a man to say to another, 'You do my killing for me', for dishonesty of that kind was beyond him. What he had not prepared for, however, and perhaps could not have prepared for, was the anatomy of carnage and death and despair he had encountered in France with the Red Cross. The Professor remembered how he told his family that all his early illusions about the glory of war had been shattered and how the aspect of the battlefield he loathed most was its sordidness. He had used the word loathed and meant it. He had seen for himself the bravery of the fighting soldier, the daunting and almost superhuman heroism of the men in the trenches, and he himself had shared the sheer courage of the men and women of the Red Cross, those who succoured the fallen and by so doing declared a protest against the suffering. When he heard the screams of the maimed and the dying, and picked up the mangled remains of those longing for the mercy of death, he was no longer the once self-assured Guardian responding with youthful enthusiasm to the old injunction 'Be strong and quit you like Men'. Siegfried had changed and been changed.

It is important to be clear about the nature of the change he had undergone. There is nothing in the record to suggest that he had converted to pacifism or that he ever thought about registering as a conscientious objector. But all the evidence at our disposal does point to the fact that he did wish to return to his life-saving medical work at the front, and, to that extent, he acknowledged that his uncharacteristic impulsive decision to enlist had been a blunder. It was not pacifism which determined his unenviable position as a private soldier in the Royal Fusiliers, but a pacifist body. He knew that a group of young Quakers, headed by Lawrence Cadbury and Philip Noel-Baker, had set up a Friends Ambulance Unit. The name Friends Ambulance Unit had arisen out of a suggestion made by Geoffrey Winthrop Young, who by now had given up his role as war correspondent, and used all his considerable organisational energy and skill in getting the Quaker project firmly established in France.

Siegfried's position was getting more and more urgent. The Friends Ambulance Unit accorded with his humanitarian stance, and he clearly wished to join it by effecting a transfer out of his regiment, Winthrop Young, with his network of contacts in high places, being recruited to help. But the November embarkation leave was already upon him. The entire family gathered for a hurried holiday together, spending five precious days based on a farmhouse named Tynohir, close to Machynlleth and a favourite retreat often used by Siegfried's parents. It was like old times again. Whether the opportunity was taken to climb Cader Idris, or any of the attractive ridges north of the wooded valleys which form the backcloth to the area, we do not know. In later years May would recall her final sight of him, seeing him off on the train at Dovey Junction, a moment very deeply etched in her memory, coloured with a strong sense of foreboding. The last goodbye was in sight of the sea to the west and the unmistakable streak of the Welsh hills. Embarkation could not be postponed, but even as he sailed from Dover to Calais on a day of faint haze, the incessant bombardment distantly audible on the other side of the water, Winthrop Young was pulling strings. On November 23rd, from the Friends Ambulance Unit at Malo, he wrote to Siegfried:

> There has been a muddle about the paper you left and the address is lost. Infinite nuisance I mind you, as by now I can only shake up Johnston by vague report. Our ambulance work has died down with the fighting; it's chiefly fever work and hospital running. But we are the unit that is going to glean what work there is, whenever it comes – and we can savour our slack time. It is difficult to get you straight into the Quakers, as they have 150 young Quakers on the waiting list. But our unit is combined with the Hon. Lionel Holland's who is the Red Cross representative here. I ran his cars for him at the front. We work in absolute harmony with him, and I could arrange for you to work with us. Roger, the head of the Red Cross Unit, and (... letter indecipherable ...) is our very good friend; and I think the best way to avoid the (... letter indecipherable ...) is for Holland to apply direct to Roger for you to be attached here to him. I am communicating with Holland about it. If you, on your side, apply to the Red Cross to be assigned here too, I feel sure the transference can be made. But I don't think Boulogne will do it.

> As you may be back at Boulogne for the new arrangements, will you arrange to come up here and see us? Let us know by wire beforehand, as I may be up at the front. Do fix this up! I can't spare you! It may be dull here too, but what there is we get, and we have further plans and contingencies in view. The big blokes are behind us!

> All luck, and let us know – Holland will probably write Roger at once (and may write you).

The *cri de coeur*, ' I can't spare you', had no homosexual overtone, but was a genuine wish to get the services of a young leader of nerve who could get things done. Winthrop Young had a true concern for the welfare of the wounded soldier, and his devoted command during the destruction of Ypres, movingly told in his *The Grace of Forgetting*, was nothing if not heroic. It is interesting that although he referred to the work of the Friends Ambulance Unit in the book, he made no mention of Siegfried.

Winthrop Young was never less than confident when he came to work things, but on this occasion he was too sanguine in thinking that Roger or Holland could pull off a transfer; perhaps they had not bargained on shadowy figures lurking at the War Office. In any event, when, in the January of

1916, the Royal Fusiliers were ordered to Festubert, Siegfried was still a serving soldier.

Siegfried's regiment had joined the bulk of the British Expeditionary Force which up to that time had remained in Flanders. Festubert was one of the dreary coalfields east of Lille, where water is found everywhere close beneath the surface and much of the line had to be constructed of sandbag barricades rather than trenches. Right across the area the Germans occupied the few commanding heights. Before the Royal Fusiliers arrived on the salient, it had already been the scene of murderous hand-to-hand fighting, engagements of extreme ferocity, gaining Festubert the reputation of being one of the more 'lively' stretches of the line. The French had come to regard the salient as *champs d'honeur* and were determined to hold it. One of those who had been present at Festubert before Siegfried was ordered there, and had experienced the conditions, was the poet and author, Robert Graves. (Siegfried and Graves had met at one of Winthrop Young's Pen-y-Pass Easter climbing parties.) In his book *Goodbye to all That* Graves gave a stark description of the appalling physical conditions endured by the soldiers. He singled out an incident of almost fantasy-like horror when the inmates of a lunatic asylum, caught between two fires, broke out and ran wildly all over the battlefield. Defences constructed by members of his battalion sank in the mud until they were engulfed. Every yard of the salient showed that death had trodden there. Festubert was a battlefield as grim as it was grotesque, where a war of attrition was carried out by both sides, with a routine of wire cutting followed by sudden raids, and with the British and French soldiers in their waterlogged dugouts close enough to the Germans to hear them speak.

Siegfried was not to be at Festubert for very long. Towards the end of January, 1916, he was sent with five companions into one of the dangerous 'island trenches' sunk in the mud in front of the main line. Their orders were to hold the trench for a period of four days; in the event, they could only do so for half that time. On the 28th, like a bolt of lightning on a mountain ridge, a German rifle grenade straddled the trench ripping Siegfried, and a young man named Thomson, apart.

A mere three hours before the fatal blast, Siegfried had written his last letter, later found in his wallet:

> The day itself passed fairly quietly, just the usual amount of 'strafing' on either side. Today is quite a fair day, for a change. We have nothing to do except sit tight in our little island and keep a watchful eye on the periscope at which a German is taking some sporting shots – We come out on Sunday night.

Poignantly, Siegfried addressed the letter to May, their bond sealed on planet Mars so long ago still holding. The warriors of Mars, in the great heroic poem of the *Aeneid*, far from wishing to escape from the God of War, openly rejoiced when their turn came to fall in battle 'on Mar's field of renown'. Renown there undoubtedly was on the gutted mud of Festubert; but there was little to rejoice about.

EPILOGUE

Siegfried is buried at Brown's Road Military Cemetery (Index No. Fr: 260, Plot 1., Grave G.3). The Cemetery is half a mile south-west of Festubert village, on the Festubert-Cuinchy road towards Beuvry. It contains the graves of 1,041 soldiers and airmen.

On February 5th, 1916, the Herfords received a letter from the Chaplain, the Rev T.W.Taylor, 5th Brigade, 2nd Division B.E.F.

Dear Professor Herford,

It is with the very deepest regret that I have to write to inform you of the death of your son, Private S.W.Herford, 2860, of the 24th Royal Fusiliers, in action on Friday last Jan 28th. I buried him on the following day in a little cemetery not far behind the firing line

I know that he was held in the very highest esteem both by his officers and his comrades, and 1 expect that his officer will also soon write to you.

As I was formerly a student at Manchester University where for two years 1 had the pleasure of attending your lectures (1906 - 1907 - 1908) I found it very difficult to write this letter to you, and beg, that as one of your former students, I may be allowed to express to you my very deepest and sincerest sympathy in your touching loss.

The news utterly devastated the Herfords. Nor was there to be much solace for them. Not until July 31st did they receive any form of official notification, and when it did come, it was from the Infantry Record Office, Hounslow, and not the War Office, detailing articles found on Siegfried and returned to his mother.

Once the news spread, letters of condolence flooded into Didsbury from every part of the country. There was a mixture of shock, disbelief, and great anguish. The climbing world was under no illusion about the magnitude of the loss that it had sustained.

Margery Eckward wrote:

I only saw the news of Siegfried's death yesterday and have been thinking of you all night. Even I, who have seen him so little in the last two years, feel that his loss makes a gap which I shall not be able to fill. I think what the Manchester Guardian said about him was absolutely true: he had a rare and very willing combina-- tion of goodness and modesty and brains. I valued his friendship very much.

George Sansom wrote:

As your son was one of my very great friends, I am writing to convey my deepest and most sincere sympathy to you for your sad loss. We had been friends for five years and during that time had spent many of the happiest hours of our lives together on the mountains. Your son was known and respected as the finest rock climber in England, and his loss will he deeply felt by a great number of his friends

A.R.Thomson wrote

He was so very different from other people one encounters in everyday life - I don't refer to climbers now - who have little or none of his generosity.

Geoffrey Winthrop Young wrote:

Siegfried was for us – besides being himself – the greatest rock climbing figure perhaps of all time: in his life already a tradition.

C. E. Montague wrote

I remember him as he stood at the top of Kern Knotts Crack, which he had just climbed for the first time, holding the rope for the second man and seeming always to he looking away when the second man climbed awkwardly, and only seeing him when he climbed better, but never for a moment relaxing his vigour or off his guard. All English rock climbers who knew him would say that he was the best of them all.

The climbing community was quick to respond to the news of Siegfried's violent death on the battlefield. C. F. Holland, who held a spiritual view of life in which the notion of the finality of death was firmly rejected, remembered his soldier brother who had also been killed in France due to a poison gas shell, and assured the Herfords that "I cannot feel unhappy about him any more that I can over my brother who had the same magnificent death". L. J. Oppenheimer, writing from the Officers Mess, Crowborough Camp in Sussex, responded in an entirely different way. He confessed, "I want to write to you to tell you what I feel, but I can say nothing but platitudes". Darwin Leighton wrote on behalf of the Fell and Rock Climbing Club:

> We as a club shall mourn his loss, not merely because of his splendid achievements in climbing, but because of his kind-heartedness and good comradeship. The memory of him will dwell with us as we again climb the hills of Lakeland that he loved so well.

A. E. Burns and J. H. Entwisle, then Joint Secretaries wrote on behalf of The Rucksack Club:

> Some of our men knew Siegfried well and were frequent companions with him on the mountains, and all of them knew him by repute and cherish the memory of a young life of singular virtue and rich promise. Nothing we could write will adequately express the honour in which your son was held by his friends, the mountain lovers. We know, nevertheless, that neither this nor anything else we can say can mitigate your grief even though he fell in so exalted a Cause. But it may help you to know that those elements of his singularly beautiful character - honour, courage, gentleness, chivalry which came to fruition in him so early and endeared him to so many will be an inspiration and a sacred memory to those who had the privilege of fellowship with him.

Eloquent though the many tributes were, it was L. J. Oppenheimer's sense of the failure of words which best caught the prevailing mood, a letter rendered all the more poignant by the fact that this able climber lost his own life in the trenches shortly after he had written. "We can only tell you of our profound fellow feeling", wrote Ernest Rhys of Everyman's Library on behalf of himself and his wife, "those of two people near to you in time, and in the cares and hopes of fathers and mothers". The

Hereford's sense of total loss was linked to the cares of mothers and fathers throughout the land, homes that awaited the arrival of a feared telegram or a Chaplain's consoling letter, as the harrowing ordeal of the Somme followed the island trenches of Festubert.

By the summer of 1919 a memorial had been installed at Platt (Unitarian) Chapel, Manchester, in the form of a window designed by Caroline Townsend. *The Inquirer* for August 9th, 1919, carried the following report:

> The window is a simple and reverent memorial. The English youth that spent itself, as Herford did, in the war, is represented in the symbolic figure of a young giant climbing rocks, with clouds below him and birds at his side and sunrise breaking on the mountain tops over his head. The designer has conventionalised the climbing boots, puttees, and costume of the figure, which is partly shadowed in green. The mountains are deep blue and purple, and the whole effect is of transfiguration.

When Platt Chapel had to be given up by the small Unitarian congregation, funds were raised to rescue the Memorial Window, and it was transferred to the Eskdale Outward Bound Mountain School where it acted as a kind of continuity with the adventure tradition Siegfried encountered at the Hermann Lietz-Schule. The unveiling ceremony at Eskdale, touchingly, was performed by May, and Austin Whittaker delivered an appreciation of his old friend.

On June 8th, 1924, the Fell and Rock Climbing Club honoured its war dead by unveiling the War Memorial tablet on the summit of Great Gable. The intimate and simple ceremony was carried out in soft rain and rolling mist on the high crest of the peak. A. W. Wakefield led, G. A. Solly read Psalm 121, Geoffrey Winthrop Young delivered a eulogy:

> By this symbol we affirm a twofold trust: that which hills only can give their children, the disciplining of strength in freedom, the freeing of the spirit through generous service, these free hills shall give again, and for all time.

Winthrop Young wrote a description of the event for Professor and Marie Herford, in which he told how the bronze tablet, to be enshrouded by the war-stained Union Jack that flew from H.M.S.Barham at the Battle of Jutland, had been lugged all the way to the top of the peak by G. M. Trevelyan and his son. The Club's statistic is a frightening one. Of the 68

Club members who served in the armed forces, no less than 19 had their names inscribed on the tablet. They are:

J. Gordon Bean	L. J. Oppenheimer
H. S. P. Blair	A. J. Pritchard
J. Clay	A. W. Rimer
J. Neville Fletcher	R. B. Sanderson
W. H. B. Grosse	H. L. Slingsby
Edmund Hartley	G. C. Turner
S. W. Herford	B. H. Whitley
Stanley Jeffcoat	J. Haworth Whitworth
E. B. Lees	Claude S. Worthington

Siegfried's is name is sandwiched between those of two friends. Stanley Jeffcoat, of course, had first introduced him to Castle Naze and taken part in the siege of Scafell. The name of Edmund Hartley is less well known. Lieut. Hartley had been a student at Brasenose College before he enlisted in the 2nd Lancashire Fusiliers. He was elected to the Fell and Rock Climbing Club in March 1914, proposed by Siegfried and seconded by C.F.Holland. Hartley was a climber of exceptional talent who had just begun to climb regularly with Siegfried.

The ceremony on the summit of Great Gable was short, simple and very moving. H.P.Cain read aloud the inscription on the Dedicatory Tablet; the assembled climbers sang 'O God, our Help in Ages past'; two boy buglers of the St. Bees School Cadets sounded the 'Last Post'. And then the climbers, in their well-worn grey or tweeds, made their orderly way down the mountain with every now and again, through the hush, the clink of boot-nails on boulders, or a word of softly spoken greeting. The damp grey mist drifted silently from the Dedicatory Tablet over to Central Buttress on Scafell.

NOTES AND REFERENCES

INTRODUCTION

1. *The Climber*, December 1966: 'Names from the Past -Siegfried Herford', Walt Unsworth
2. *Manchester University Magazine*, 1916

PLANET MARS

1. *Sunday's Child*, Catherine T. Herford, Lindsey Press, 1949. Siegfried's cousin.
2. *The Dragon*, University College of Wales, Summer 1931.
3. *The Inquirer*, May 9th, 1931
4. *Dictionary of National Biography 1931-1940,* Oxford University Press, 1949
5. *In Memoriam Siegfried Wedgwood Herford*, a compendium privately printed by the Herford family, 1917.
6. *I do what I like*, W. A. Darlington, Macdonalds, 1947.

DIDSBURY AND UNITARIANISM

1. *The Unitarian Contribution to Social Progress in England*, Raymond Holt, George Allen and Unwin. 1938
2. *The Concise Oxford Dictionary of the Christian Church*, Ed: E. A. Livingston. Oxford University Press, 1977
3. *Platt (Unitarian) Chapel 1700-1950*, Edwin Swindells, published by the Chapel.

QUIT YOU LIKE MEN

1. The Wilhelm von Fellenberg referred to should not be confused with the eminent Swiss geologist and mountaineer; Edmund von Fellenberg. It was to Edmund, and not Wilhelm, that Edward Whymper wrote the earliest extant account of the Matterhorn accident, on July 25th, 1865.
2. *Lady Barn House and the Work of W. H. Herford*, W. C. R. Hicks, Manchester University Press, 1916
3. *Mid-Victorian Britain 1851-70*, Geoffrey Best, Wiedenfeld and Nicholson, 1971.

4. *Snowdon Biography,* Geoffrey Winthrop Young, Geoffrey Sutton and Wilfrid Noyce. J. M. Dent & Sons Ltd
5. *Ibid* In Memoriam
6. *The Manchester Grammar School 1515-1965*, J.A. Graham and B.A. Phythian, Manchester University Press, 1965.
7. *Adventures in Holiday Making*, T.Arthur Leonard, Holiday Fellowship, 1934.
8. *Fell & Rock Climbing Club Journal* 1916.

BICYCLING

1. We possess no details about what maps to North Wales Siegfried or his father used. We do know how the Professor was given to meticulous planning, and there was a guide available to him: *The Roads of England and Wales* by Charles Howard (Letts and Son, 1882). a compendium 'specially adapted for the bicycle tourist'.
2. Sadly, the historic photographs taken by Siegfried on Snowdon have not been traced.
3. Herman Holmann quoted in *The Hitler Youth*, H.W. Koch, Macdonald and James. 1975.

A MOUNTAIN LEGACY

1. *Ibid* F & R.C.C.J.
2. Wilhelm von Fellenberg did not always limit his Hofwyl school parties to alpine passes. On August 8th, 1842, four boys on a school expedition – John Barwell, a boy named Lushington, and the brothers William and Valentine Smith – made the first ascent of the Riffelhorn above the Gornergrat at Zermatt. See – *Guide des Alpes Valaisannes* Vol 3a 1952.
3. *Castle Howell School Record,* Ed: Rev. D.Davies, Lancaster, 1888.
4. *Oxford Mountaineering Essays*, Ed: Arnold Lunn, Edwin Arnold, 1912.

A MANCHESTER CLIMBER

1. *Ludwig Wittgenstein: The Duty of Genius*, Ray Monk, Vintage, 1991
2. *The Climbers' Club Journal*, February 1913.
3. *Fell & Rock Climbing Club Journal*, 1936: 'A short History of

Lakeland Climbing', H.M.Kelly and J.H.Doughty.

4. *A Short History of the Rucksack Club 1902-1939*, Philip Brockbank, privately printed, 1977.

5. *Ibid.* F. & R.C.C.J.

6. *Ibid.* Brockbank.

7. *High Peak*, E.Byne and G.Sutton, Secker and Warburg, 1966.

8. Vin Desmond was killed in a tragic accident in January 1962, when a snow cornice broke under him during a traverse of the Berwyns.

9. *Rucksack Club Journal*, 1915, 'Ilam Rock', by A.R. Thomson.

10 *The English Outcrops*, Walt Unsworth, Gollancz Ltd., 1964.

THE HOME CRAGS OF ERYRI

1. *Welsh Rock*, T.Jones and G.Milburn, Pic Publications, 1986.

2. *Rock Climbing in Wales,* Ron James, Constable, 1970.

3. *Climbing Days*. Dorothy Pilley, G.Bell and Sons, 1935.

A FELL AND ROCK MAN

1. *Fell & Rock Climbing Club Journal* , 1981.

2. *Climbing in Wasdale before the First World War*, George Sansom, Castle Cary Press 1982. The Rudyard Kipling quotation is taken from 'The Ballad of East and West', written in 1889.

3. The Abraham film is available on video, *Century on the Crags: The Story of Rock Climbing in the English Lake District,* Striding Edge Limited, Wasdale.

4. Some climbers have long memories. A.S.Pigott, in his Obituary of Wilson Hey, referred to the occasion when 'Siegfried Herford capriciously removed the chockstone'. Capricious is a bit strong from a man not without sin himself. See – *Rucksack Club Journal*, 1956.

5. Geoffrey Winthrop Young, in an historical introduction to the 1939 edition of the *Lliwedd* guide-book, made it clear that the Climbers' Club intended to extend its guide-book actitvity to the Lake District prior to the First World War. He wrote: 'I had, further, arranged with the Oxford Press for the series to be extended to the Lakes. Herford undertook the first of these, for Scafell, and it was in the course of the preliminary work for this guide – interrupted by the war – that his explorations of the Pinnacle Face were made and the

Flake Crack ascended.' Young provided no date for when Siegfried agreed to work on the preparation of a guide-book, but by implication, if the preliminary work was interrupted by the war, it must have been late. Young would seem to have compressed the chronology of events. Siegfried and Sansom made no reference to a guide-book in their 'The Climbs of Scafell Pinnacle' article in the 1912 issue of the *Fell & Rock Journal,* and, indeed, they made no reference of any kind to a guide-book, any more did Holand. One has to wonder whether Young's memory was fully on the mark in this instance. Siegfried had clearly been exploring the Scafell massif well before his climbing could have been interrupted by the war.

6. I have not been able to discover whether Brunskill's article was ever published; I suspect not. He sent a typed copy to Siegfried for comment. Siegfried objected to the title, the opening sentence, and added six emendations to the text.

7. A reference to O.G.Jones's *Rock-Climbing in the English District.* G.P.Abraham and Sons, 1900, page 87.

8. Hopkinson's Cairn was erected in 1887, when the three younger Hopkinson brothers, Charles, Edward and Albert along with their cousin W. N.Tribe, forced a way down to the top of Scafell Pinnacle. What Brunskill referred to was a failed attempt in the December of the same year, led by Charles Hopkinson, to reach the Cairn from below.

TWO FRIENDSHIPS

1. *Mountains with a Difference*, Geoffrey Winthrop Young, Eyre and Spottiswoode, 1951

2. *Geoffrey Winthrop, Young: Poet, Mountaineer, Educator*, Alan Hankinson, Hodder and Stoughton, 1995.

3. *A Tramp to Brighton: de Profundis ad Suprema*, E.S.Kennedy; Simpson, Marshall, Hamilton, Kent & Co., Exeter and Exmouth, 1892. A small book with a niche in the history of penology.

4. The Discharged Prisoners Aid Society, precursor to the present National Association for the Care and Resettlement of Offenders.

CENTRAL BUTTRESS

1. *Hard Rock*, Ed: Ken Wilson, Hart-Davies MacGibben, 1974.
2. *Ibid*. Kelly & Doughty.
3. The full text of the letter is reproduced in Sansom's *Wasdale*, pages 73-76.
4. A sad postscript has to be added to the story of the chockstone. On Saturday, June 4th,1994, Iain Newman and Rob Cobbeld, two highly experienced climbers from I.M.Marsh Outdoor Pursuits College at Liverpool, were on Flake Crack. Iain Newman placed a runner round the chockstone, following normal practice, and just as he began to layback up the Flake, the historic chockstone dislodged itself from the crack, hitting his right leg and severing the main artery. Despite most valiant efforts by Rob Cobbeld himself, and those of the rescue team, Iain Newman's life could not be saved. Present climbers are reminded that the chockstone is not in situ.

THE WATZMANN AND BEYOND

1. On August 16th, 1888, after only four seasons of intensive climbing Georg Winkler was buried by an avalanche at the foot of the Weisshorn in the Valais. His body drifted down locked in the glacier and emerged for recovery in 1958.
2. *Alpine Journal 1969*: 'In Memoriam' Hans Brantschen 1888-1968.
3. *On High Hills*. Geoffrey Winthrop Young, Methuen, 1924.
4. *Alpine Journal 1916*: New Climbs in 1914: The Gspaltenhorn Ridge.
5. *Alpine Journal 1920*: 'Some Notes on the South-West or Rote Zähne of the Gspaltenhorn', by Paul Montandon. With three illustrations showing the formidable nature of the towers. Winthrop Young, in his own Alpine Journal article (Note 4 above) was incorrect to attribute the second ascent of the Rote Zähne to Montandon; this was done by J.Bernet and J.Rumf, of Kienthal. Montandon made the third ascent.
6. *Ibid*; Hankinson.

THE GOD OF MARS

1. *Somme*, Lyn MacDonald, Penguin Books 1983. Brilliantly documented and extremely moving.
2. *The Face of Battle*, John Keegan, Pimlico Edition, 1995.

APPENDIX ONE

GLOSSARY OF CLIMBING TERMS USED IN THE BOOK.

Abseil	A rapid method of descent using the rope to slide down.
Arête	The ridge as opposed to the face of a mountain.
Belay	A projection of rock around which a rope may be placed to protect a party. Also the verb,'to belay'. Anchor. When a climber is securely belayed, he/she is said to be well protected.
Chimney	A large crack which the climber can get into.
Contouring	Walk across a hillside, usually at the same height.
Couloir	A French word applicable to the Alps and roughly equivalent to the English gully i.e. a rift or furrow scooped out between two buttresses caused by erosion.
Exposure	Drop beneath a climber. Openness.
Fissure	A narrow crack.
Gardening	The removal of turf or plants on a rock climb.
Gendarme	A rock tower situated on a ridge and usually barring the way. Sometimes called a 'tooth' or a 'pinnacle'.
Girdle	Traversing the whole distance across the face of a cliff or crag.
Glissade	A fast, controlled slide, using an ice-axe for direction or speed
Hut	In Britain, as opposed to the Alps, a self-catering bunkhouse privately owned by a climbing club.
Ice-Axe	A wooden or metal shaft with a head fashioned into an adze or blade and the end into the ferruled spike.
Left/Right	As a climber faces a mountain or a crag. On the descent as facing downwards.
Length	The length of rope between one climber and another.
Nails	Boot nailing. During the period covered by this book the commonest nail was the mugger special edging nails made of soft iron, which permitted rock to bite into them. Round about the end of 1910 a new type of nail, the tricouni, was used. This had three flattened prongs and was fixed round the edge of the boot. By about 1960 nails had more or less ceased to be used.
Piton	In English a peg. A steel leaf, some with rings in one end, driven into rocks to providesecurity(belay) where no natural safety projection exists. Pegs come in various

	sizes and thicknesses. Also called an 'aid'.
Pitch	Distance between two stances.
Run Out	Length of rope required between two stances.
Rubbers	Rubber shoes. Plimsolls. Used on dry rock and slabs to enhance friction. In 1912, Siegfried Herford and John Laycock used a type of rope-soled shoe called *scarpetti* on Alphabet Slab, Glyder Fach.
Snaplink	More correctly karabiner. An oval or D-shaped metal link which opens by means of a spring clip. Main belay karabiners have a screw gate so as to lock the running rope. Used for abseiling.
Stance	Place to stop and preferably to stand and even more preferably with a belay. The 'Oval' on Scafell is a famous stance.
Standard	Agreed technical grade of a route – or move – found in a guide book, i.e. 'Difficult' or 'Very Severe'.
Tricouni	Nails for climbing boots with sharp teeth.

APPENDIX TWO

ITEMS RELEVANT TO S.W.HERFORD IN THE FELL AND ROCK CLIMBING CLUB JOURNAL

1911. Club Meets Page 260: Herford and Laycock on July meet at Coniston. Herford on 2nd ascent of Easter Gully, Dow Crag, with McConechy.

1912. *The Climbs on Scafell Pinnacle* by Herford and Sansom.
Jones's Route – picture by Brunskill.
The Traverse of Scafell Crags by Herford.
Days in Arfon by Laycock. About Herford in Wales.
Climbs Old and New by Herford and Sansom. First ascent of Kern Knotts West Buttress; re Kern Knotts Crack see note by Editor; Napes Needle Variation.

1913. *Two Famous Dolomite Climbs* by Herford: Winkler and Fiinffingerspitze.
Recent First Ascents by Laycock. Picture of Herford on Zig~Zag Climb.
The Sixth Annual Dinner: Coniston. Herford at his first Dinner, November 2nd, 1912.
Iron Crag Gully by A.R.Thomson. Picture by Laycock.
Woodhead's Climb – Herford and Jeffcoat on Scafell Pinnacle.

Some Gritstone Climbs – Review of Laycock's guide book.

1914   List 'Members with the Colours'. *Scafell Central Buttress*
    by Sansom.
    The Doctrine of Descent by Herford.
    Impressions of Skye by Laycock. Picture of Herford on
    the Cioch.
    Walker's Gully by C.F.Holland.
    A Year with the Fell and Rock Club. Herford and Jeffcoat
    at the 1913 Annual Dinner.
    Climbs Old and New Notes by Herford on Stack Ghyll,
    Buttermere; Birkness Gully; Birkness Chimney; Yew Crag
    Gully.
    Page 96. Note on time taken by Herford from Sun
    Hotel, Coniston, to Dow Crag.

1916   *In Memoriam* Laycock's Obituary of Herford.
    Roll of Honour Contains a reference to Herford.

1917   *In Memoriam* Jeffcoat's Obituary. Hartley's Obituary.

1919   Record of Honour Service: Roll of Honour

1921.   *The Great Central Buttress of Scafell* by Holland: a
    panegyric of Herford.

1924.   *Unveiling the War Memorial Tablet* by Palmer.

1931.   *The Bonded Ware'ous*e by Holland. Herford in the Lakes
    and Skye.

1937.   *Rupert in the Chair* by Holland. Reference to Herford.

1961.   *In Memoriam* Laycock's Obituary.

1968.   *In Memoriam* Holland's Obituary.

1981   *In Memoriam* Sansom's Obituary

APPENDIX THREE

S.W.HERFORD'S COPY OF 'THE COMPLETE MOUNTAINEER'

Herford marked up his copy of George Abraham's book *The Complete Mountaineer* with lists of climbs and annotations. The lists, particularly, are hard to fathom at times, and they are certainly no substitute for a proper logbook, but all the markings repay study because they shed a little more light on Herford's climbing.

The Front Cover

The front cover of the book contains a recording of various visits Herford made to gritstone outcrops. We know his list is not complete. Wharncliffe Crags, Black Rocks, Cratcliffe Tor, and Laddow Rocks are given a mention; but Castle Naze, the Roaches and Hen Cloud are not. There is a note of interest concerning Kinder Downfall, from which we learn that he was out climbing on the Downfall in November 1909, in other words, before his meeting with John Laycock, although there is no reference to the meeting itself nor to the climbs he did on the Downfall.

The front cover also includes a long list of climbs in Wales. Quite what the list means it is difficult to be sure, for there are no ticks or dates indicating he had climbed the routes referred to, although we know for certain he had done many of them. Again, the list is far from being complete, for it fails to mention several routes we know he did climb.

The Main Text

Herford's annotations in the main text are revealing in the sense that they show how firmly he made up his own mind on climbing matters.

Page 53: Herford scribbled on the picture showing the beginning of Kern Knotts Crack: 'The direct ascent of the crack from the very bottom is more difficult'. Page 139: Under the picture of Napes Needle: NB 'Keep right leg outside crack, otherwise jammed'. Still good advice.

Page 155: Herford and George Abraham were friends, and climbed together on several occasions, but this did not prevent Herford from correcting his friend when he thought it necessary. He was obviously not satisfied with Abraham's description of Shamrock Gully on Pillar Rock, and we find the following substitution: 'The pitch consists of one huge, wedged boulder, and is about 35 feet high'. He then added a question mark after Abraham's 'less severe', for master technician though he was, he never allowed rock the benefit of the doubt. From Herford's list on the back cover of the book, we discover that on July 1st, 1911, he did the ordinary route of Shamrock Gully and then followed this by a 'new route', the precise line of which we do not know.

Page 187: With reference to the Horned Crag Climb we find the comment: 'L.Salt killed here 28-3-1920'.

Page 206: On the margin of the picture of the Upper Cave Pitch,

Great Gully, Craig yr Ysfa, Herford noted: 'Very stiff 10ft pitch'. In a letter to his father, dated August 1912, describing his solo ascent of Great Gully, he said he found the cave pitch 'the most interesting though by no means the hardest part of the course'.

The Rear Cover

This is dominated by a tabulation of climbs in the Lake District, a list which is far more informative than the one Herford did for Wales, for a goodly number of the climbs are ticked, and dated as having been done. Again, the list is by no means complete, for it begins in 1909, thus leaving out his ascent of Napes Needle the previous year, and anything else he might have climbed at the same time. By ending in 1911 it not only excludes his important later routes, but also everything done during the ubiquitous year of 1912 when he got in 100 days of climbing. Still, it is a revealing list, showing the way he worked and probed a given area. The following routes, with his comments, are those listed as having been climbed:

Ticked But Undated

Collier's Climb
West Climb Pillar Rock
Arrowhead Ridge Traverse from East Side
Deep Ghyll Ordinary Route
Pavey Ark Gullies
Sergeant Crag Gully – Direct Route
C Gully of the Screes
Scafell Pinnacle direct from Lord's Rake
Oblique Chimney
Doe Crag Great Gully
Keswick Brothers' Climb
Engineer's Chimney, Gable Crag.
Screes Great Gully (Direct)

Ticked and Dated

06-08-09	Broad Strand
10-08-09	Deep Ghyll by the West Wall Traverse
10-08-09	Scafell Pinnacle - Easy way up
10-08-09	Professor's Chimney
19-08-09	Napes Needle
19-08-09	Needle Ridge
19-O8-09	Kern Knotts Chimney

22-08-09   Kern Knotts Chimney

Nothing listed for 1910

27-06-11   Eagle's Nest Ridge - Ordinary way
28-06-11   Scafell Pinnacle by Deep Ghyll
28-06-11   Moss Ghyll by Direct Finish
29-06-11   Pillar Rock by Right Pisgah
29-06-11   Pillar Rock (by North Face)
30-06-11   Scafell Pinnacle by Deep Ghyll
01-07-11   Shamrock Gully (Ordinary Route)
01-07-11   Shamrock Gully (New Route)
02-07-11   Kern Knotts West Chimney
02-07-11   Kern Knotts Crack (rope from above)
05-07-11   North Face of Pillar (by hand Traverse).
06-07-11   Keswick Brother's climb - Variation Finish.
06-07-11   Pisgah Ridge by the Tennis Court Ledge
08-07-11   Doe Crag Intermediate Gully
09-07-11   Doe Crag Central Chimney
15-08-11   Kern Knotts Crack
30-09-11   North West Climb Pillar Rock
30-09-11   Walker's Gully Pillar Rock
31-12-11   Walker's Gully Pillar Rock

The rear cover, in addition to the List of climbs, also contains a partial description of the middle section of a 160ft severe. Quite what it is is hard to say, for it is difficult to make it tally with any known route, but it would seem that Brunskill was on the climb, and Herford noted that it was done in stockinged feet

Reading Herford's list is a bit like travelling back in time with the beneficent feel of classic rock, and the ghost of O.G.Jones lurking somewhere in the background. It is not the list of the rounded master Herford would become, but that of a young man still feeling his way, testing his faculties and technique, first tackling Kern Knotts Crack on a top rope and then leading it a month later. He was a bold climber, but prudent. We are given a glimpse of the engineer's mind at work, the systematic and regular returns to the same place so as to familiarise himself with the nature of the terrain, Scafell Pinnacle or Pillar Rock, analysing the problems and then applying a solution with a silent self-confidence. In 1909, he looked at the easy side of Scafell Pinnacle, looking at the obvious first as an engineer would do, and by 1912 he had penetrated to its inmost depths. Herford's markings and lists all make for a unique copy of Abraham's book.

164

INDEX